PERF1
CV

Terry O'Brien is a best-selling author, columnist, consultant and motivational trainer. He is highly sought-after in the corporate as well as academic world, and has been training managers and providing counselling and consultancy over the past couple of decades. Author of hugely popular books on motivation, effective change and all that is 'un-Google-able', his writings focus on skill development and communication techniques. Terry O'Brien is a firm believer that 'infotainment' is a must for content to be effective, and his books are all about the three 'R's: Read, Record and Recall.

OTHER TITLES IN THE SERIES

PERFECT

CV

Get it right every time

Terry O'Brien

RUPA

Published by
Rupa Publications India Pvt. Ltd 2017
7/16, Ansari Road, Daryaganj
New Delhi 110002

Sales centres:
Allahabad Bengaluru Chennai
Hyderabad Jaipur Kathmandu
Kolkata Mumbai

ISBN: 978-81-291-4538-3

First impression 2017

10 9 8 7 6 5 4 3 2 1

Printed by Nutech Print Services, New Delhi

Typeset by Chetan Sharma

Contents

Contents

Introduction

A Curriculum Vitae (CV) presents a record of your qualities, skills and experience to employers, so that your suitability for a particular job can be assessed. In Latin, 'Curriculum Vitae' means 'the way your life has run' and 'Résumé' is the French word for 'summary'.

For a job seeker, a CV is a document outlining pertinent information needed by a prospective employer; it is to enable the employer to assess quickly whether or not a meeting would be worthwhile. If the employer likes the CV, it may lead to an interview. If not, you and the selector will have both been saved the time and effort of an interview.

Perfect CV can help you compile or suggest ways to improve your CV.

When compiling a CV, remember it should be well-designed and not too cramped—appearance is important because the first impression counts.

Leave spaces between sections and at the top, bottom and sides of the page. A CV should usually be about two pages but no longer than three sides of A4 size paper—using bullet points is a good way of ensuring that it is concise.

Always print your CV on good quality A4 paper; ensure that the font size is not too big or small; use graphics only if they are relevant and add value to your CV, however, they should be avoided.

Try to prioritise and allocate space according to the importance of the information and be selective when choosing examples of duties performed in previous employment. Also, if a company has requested a job application to be completed in order to apply, it is not acceptable to send your CV.

A CV should include these details.

Basic information

Personal details: A simple heading, such as your name, usually works best. This can be followed by your address, telephone number and email address.

Personal profile: This section is where you make your first impression and sell yourself to the employers. You need to write a few lines that describe you as a person and highlight your strengths.

Skills and abilities: In this section, you need to tell employers the key skills and abilities that you possess. Think of the skills that you have improved over time, through work or training. It's also important to include skills and abilities that you use in your everyday life and might also be of use at work, for instance, speaking, listening, organising and time management skills.

Employment history: Start by putting down the details of your last job, then work backwards. Include any voluntary community work that you have done.

Keep the details of your duties brief but make sure you don't leave any out. For example:

- Answering the telephone/taking messages
- Controlling incoming and outgoing post
- Giving information to clients

Don't think any job is mundane or irrelevant; make sure that the information provided is relevant to the particular job or type of work that interests you.

Education and training: Name and location of school(s) attended should be provided here with brief details of qualifications gained and grades achieved. The year when qualifications were gained can also be included.

If you finished school but did not gain any formal qualifications thereafter, mention the schools you have attended and the examination taken.

If you did not finish school, nor did you gain any qualifications, you should mention the school attended and focus on your experience.

If you have studied at any colleges or universities, the name and location of each institution should be given here. Details should be given of any qualifications gained, including the year and grade.

Additional training or skills developed: This section should be used to offer information on any other qualification achieved or any relevant training courses that you have attended (including the year). This could include languages, computing skills, vocational qualification etc., and also include one-day courses and short work-based trainings.

Additional information

Do state any other information that you feel is relevant, and which you cannot fit into one of the previous sections.

Interests and hobbies: Provide details of your hobbies and any other leisure activities, such as travel, membership of organisations or clubs and any positions of responsibility. If it's an everyday hobby, make it stand out. Your interests can tell a potential employer a great deal about your personality.

References

If you are short of space on your CV or you do not have permission from referees, you can write this statement: 'References available upon request'.

- If you do put your referees on the CV, make sure you have asked their permission. If it is a person from one of your previous organisations, ensure that the person still works there. Include his/her name, job title, full address, post code and telephone number.

- Usually it is preferred that you have at least two work references—one from one of your previous employers and another from one of the educational institutes that you have attended. The referees must not be your family members.

Writing a personal statement

A critical aspect of creating an effective CV is writing a personal statement; sometimes called a profile or career summary, it enables the recruiter to quickly identify the strategic value you can add to their organisation. Your CV should be a self-marketing document aimed at persuading the recruiter to interview you, and your personal statement is indeed a critical part of making this happen.

Many candidates struggle with writing the personal statement but it isn't as difficult as you think it may be. A well-written statement can be between 50–200 words; it is very important not to ramble.

Remember: The covering letter is to give interesting and engaging information.

It's important to read the job specifications carefully and ensure that not only your skills and experience match the requirement but that you reflect this in your personal statement. You may write in the first person because the CV is all about you and your skills. This, however, doesn't mean that you begin each sentence with 'I'.

As a general rule, it's best to break the statement into these three sections.
- Who you are
- What you can bring to the table
- Your career aim

Here are a few key points for writing a dynamic and interesting personal statement.

- Get straight to the point. Avoid lengthy descriptions and make your testimonies punchy and informative.
- Keep it between 50–200 words.
- If you have enough space, use 1.5 line spacing to make you statement easier to read.
- Match person and job specifications with a well-written copy.
- Read your profile out loud to ensure it reads well.
- Don't mix first- and third-person sentences.

Other essential resources:

- Read at least three good cover letters.
- Select your CV template: graduates, career changers and ladder climbers.
- Prepare the questions to be asked at the end of your interview.
- Learn how to write a CV when you lack relevant work experience.

Do you need a CV profile?

The main reason for writing a profile is that it provides the kind of explanation you would give if you were presenting your CV in person. You'd probably say something like, 'Before you read this, let me tell you...' What you're really saying is, 'Please notice this...', 'Don't look at that...' and 'Let me tell you the things I didn't mention...'

Usually, you won't be in the room when someone reads your CV, so it should tell its own story. The profile draws immediate attention to the things you want an employer to see—it's your way of telling the reader what to notice.

The profile is the hardest part of your CV, and since it draws on your very best evidence, you probably can't compose it until the rest of your CV has taken shape. A CV will contain about 50–60 examples taken from a timeline that spans thousands of events. Your job, eventually, is to filter these so the best information is what hits the reader first. You'll find that you work out what gems to lead with, by building up bullet points gradually, starting with jobs you did some time back. This book is based on the premise of experience and learning; it makes little claim to originality or depth.

Indeed, here is all you need to get it right every time!

Who You Are

The opening should allow the recruiter to quickly identify where you are coming from, that you have industry experience (something that may be in the selection criteria) and core transferable skills. This, in itself, could be enough for your opening statement, but it can be expanded upon with some additional information.

A career aim, personal statement or profile can be a useful way of showcasing an interest and skills for a particular career on your CV, especially if you have no relevant qualification or work experience. When a profile is used, it can be assumed that a personal statement could have been used in its place. A profile is only part of a CV.

• Career objective • Career aim • Career aspiration • Career goal	• Personal profile • Personal statement • Key attributes • About me…	Preferred title: Profile
• Focuses on the type of work you wish to do	• Focuses on your skills and achievements • Tells an employer who you are and what you can do for them • Steer away from vague skills	• Short and to the point • Contains a sentence or two about the type of work you are aiming for • A few lines about the attributes which make you suitable for the role
	• Focuses more on specific competencies, such as persuading, negotiating, lateral thinking, time management, planning, decision-making, business awareness and other skills	• You can even call it nothing at all. If it's placed at the start of the CV, you can just have an un-named paragraph.

- It's not necessary to have a profile but if you do, it must be lively and succinct!
- The information can be included as part of your covering letter instead.
- It can be a useful summary, particularly if you are sending your CV to recruitment agencies where a letter may become detached.
- A covering letter tends to be most used and effective for fields where there is a lot of competition—PR, advertising, management consultancy, media and event management. Hence, your CV really needs to stand out from the crowd.

Difference between a profile and a covering letter

A profile is a short introduction to your CV, whereas a covering letter is a one-page letter going into much more detail about why you are suitable for a specific job and organisation. There will inevitably be some overlap in content, so you may use synonyms (use a thesaurus) or write the content from a slightly different perspective.

Because your profile will be on all your CVs, you normally just mention the particular job sector you are applying for, for instance, publishing. A covering letter is normally used to apply for a specific advertised vacancy and so will focus on a particular job, for instance, editorial assistant in a particular publishing company. Sometimes you may send out a speculative covering letter with your CV; here, the focus will be broad, just like in the profile, as you don't know which jobs might be available.

Profile Content	Covering Letter Content
• State the job sector you're applying for (Example: Publishing).	• State the job you're applying for (Example: Editorial assistant).
• Summarise your strengths. • State when you're available to work.	• Mention from where you found out about the job (advertisement in *The Telegraph* etc.; organisations like to know which of their advertising sources are more successful).
	• State when you're available to start work.
	• Answer why you're interested in that type of work.
	• State why the company attracts you. (If it's a smaller company, say you prefer to work for a smaller organisation.)
	• Summarise your strengths and how they might be an advantage to the organisation.
	• Relate your skills to the job.
	• Mention any dates on which you won't be available for an interview.
	• Thank the employer and say you look forward to hearing from them soon.

What if I have no idea of what job I wish to go into?

In this case, it might be better not to include a profile. An unfocused profile is worse than none at all. However, a carefully worded summary of your key strengths and attributes will enhance your CV.

Length and placement of the 'Key strengths' section

- This section should be no longer than six lines. It must be short, positive and should highlight your key strengths, skills, experience and interests. It is meant to be an appetizer rather than to give the employer indigestion! There will be time to elaborate and give evidence for these strengths, which will be covered in the CV.

- Place the statement at the start of the CV. Sometimes, the statement is placed halfway through the CV or at the end. This will defeat the objective, which is to give a concise introduction to your aim and skills.

- Start with a short description, for instance, 'A highly motivated graduate who has just completed a Law degree from the University of Delhi.'

- General statements, such as 'I have good teamworking and communication skills', send selectors to sleep as they appear so frequently. Use a thesaurus to look for better words to use. Use action words to brighten up the content.

- Analyse your core strengths. A profile is a sales tool. It is a concise summary of why an employer should hire you, so you should include brief details about your major selling points, especially those that are important in the job you are applying for.

- CVs sent to recruitment agencies can benefit from a statement, as a covering letter may become detached. Some agencies send you for unsuitable jobs; a 'Career aim' can prevent this. However, the 'Career aim' needs to be fairly broad or you may find your CV being submitted for fewer vacancies.

What You Can Bring To The Table

Utilising excellent communication skills, you could state how you developed and maintained successful working relationships with both internal and external staff.

To convey that you've got what they need, you should talk about the things you're good at, and how these are relevant to the role that they need filled. Focusing on your strengths—what you're good at and can bring to the table—will help to get this message across. Do not focus on the parts of the job that are your weaknesses. Don't even bring them up. Dwelling on what you can't bring to the table will only hurt you. For all you know, they've already decided that those specific details in the job description aren't really important. If they bring up your weaknesses, discuss them; but then return to what you can bring to the table. When confronted with this situation in an interview, everyone has to show his/her value!

What value do you bring to the table? Are you showing value in your current role? Better still, if you are job hunting, how are you showing value during those interviews?

Merely showing up for an interview and answering a few questions does not bring value.

What is your value statement? If you were asked during an interview what your value statement was, what would your reply be? If you are already in the organisation, what value are you bringing to your role?

We all like to believe that we are important and valuable, but have you ever thought about how to measure them? Today, you must demonstrate your worth regardless of how you feel about it. If you are in the 'job search' mode, what value will you bring to this role?

You must bring it alive!

You need to bring your intrinsic value to the table.

- Personality
- Affiliations
- Contributions
- Experiences
- Relationships
- Skills, Knowledge and Abilities (KSAs)

Career Aim

Aim high in your career but stay humble at heart.

State where you can bring immediate and strategic value and develop your current skill set further.

After your name, the first section that hiring managers see on your résumé is 'Career objective'. A well-written 'Career objective' will compel the hiring manager to keep reading your résumé.

Here are a few guidelines for writing a career objective, depending on your level of expertise.

If written correctly, it is a smart way to capture the attention of the hiring manager. Unfortunately, most people misunderstand what 'Career objective' is supposed to say.

It is a short blurb telling the hiring manager what skills, knowledge and abilities you have that will help the company achieve its goals.

It must not say what you want from the company and how that will help your career.

If you follow this rule, your 'Career objective' will naturally be strong. Here is how you can get concrete ideas about how to write yours.

Career Objective For A High School Student (With Zero Experience)

If you do not have professional experience or a college degree, you may be hoping to land an entry-level job, apprenticeship or internship.

In your career objective, you'll need to emphasise general traits about your character, personality and work ethics that would make you a valuable employee.

You can do this by splitting the objective into three sentences.

One: Self-introduction, mentioning your strongest (provable) traits

Two: Telling the hiring manager which role you want to fill

Three: Emphasising that you are reliable and have company goals in mind

Here's an example of a career objective for a high school résumé.

'A hardworking student with proven leadership and organisational skills, I am a dedicated team player, who pays attention to detail and can be relied upon to help your company achieve its goals.'

This student claims to have leadership and organisational skills as his/her main traits, as well as high grades.

Each of these will need to be proven later in the résumé, along with other information, such as the applicant is an elected member of the student council or has helped organise events at school.

Rule of thumb

Don't just give nice-sounding words to describe yourself; make sure that the traits you claim to have are actually reflected in your résumé. You'll need to think about what personality traits and strengths you exhibited in the activities you participated in (at school).

Here's a list of activities and their associated character traits.

School Monitorship	Associated Character Traits
Student monitor	Leadership, management, organisation
Sports	Team player, disciplined, strategic
Theatre/Art	Public speaking, presentation and interpersonal skills

| Various clubs | Active, friendly, enthusiastic |
| Academics | Analytical, hardworking, fast learner |

Relate Career objective to the role

A manager looking to hire an intern in the finance department will be less interested in your public speaking abilities than analytical skills. However, a restaurant manager might be more interested in your interpersonal skills than your analytical abilities.

Importance of writing a 'Career objective'

In many résumés, 'Career objectives' is positioned at a prominent place, either at the beginning of the résumé or at the end.

This gives the reader a quick idea as to what the professional is seeking. With this, the reader can make a quick decision as to whether the company can really provide what the professional is seeking.

Furthermore, with the changing times, working for a company has become a give-and-take relationship, where both the professional and the company work with each other based on mutual understanding. Hence, under such conditions, it is crucial that the professional as well as the company are open about what they expect from each other, from the very beginning. Due to these reasons, if a career objective is not listed, the reader may think that the professional does not know what he or she wants and is undecided, or is generally not knowledgeable.

Another aspect that one must keep in mind is that the 'Career objectives' should be written in a style and language that complies with the rest of the résumé. Sometimes, a person applying for a job pays a lot of attention to the entire résumé but writes the 'Career objectives' in a hurry. Therefore, the connection between the résumé and the objectives is lost. This creates a strange scenario for the interviewer and it could be one of the reasons why the company may not call you for an interview!

Sample career objectives

You should make sure that your 'Career objectives' section does not ramble on about your ambitions. Make sure that the 'Career objectives' is simple, crisp and to the point.

Of course, the most important aspect to remember is that you should be truthful and honest in writing down what you want and what you seek.

WRITING CAREER OBJECTIVES

Now that we know that career objectives form an important part of the profile, we should also find out what has to be marked out as a career objective.

Pursue A Career In Your Profession

The first aspect of getting it right is that they should be in line with the job that you have applied for. For example, if you have applied for a job in an IT company, you should make sure that your career objectives reflect that you have taken academic degrees and have always wanted to pursue a career in the IT field. In the same manner, if you are trying to pursue marketing or even a creative field, you should make sure that the 'Career objectives' reflects the same.

The bottom line ought to be: Build a long-term career in 'your profession' with opportunities for growth.

People working in the business of technology should use 'Career objectives' to speak about the technologies that they would like to learn about.

Along with technology, the professional should make it clear that he or she would be more than interested in learning new skills that the job will offer them. One should also add that learning new technologies would be beneficial for the individual as well as the company. The essence is to keep up with the cutting-edge technologies.

Senior level

If you are trying to join a company at a senior level, it would be a good idea to mention the same in the 'Career objectives'. You may say that you are looking for a company that offers you the perfect environment for employing your abilities and experience for the betterment of the business, the company and, therefore, for your own career.

'...to use my skills in the best possible way for achieving the company's goals...'

Entry level

Additionally, try to keep the 'Career objectives' practical and not overly ambitious. In the professional world, being logical is not only practical, but it is also a very good idea. Therefore, if you are seeking an entry-level position, the 'Career objectives' should state that you are looking to join a stable company that would give you a chance to learn and, therefore, enhance your job profile.

'…to enhance my professional skills in a dynamic and stable workplace.'

Problem Solving

The 'Career objectives' may speak about the chance of solving problems in a creative manner that the position would offer to the person selected for the job.

'To solve problems in an effective/creative manner in a challenging position…'

'Seeking a responsible job with an opportunity to learn from professional challenges…'

Here are a few more examples of 'Career objectives' for different situations.

New joiner in an IT company

'To gain employment with a company or an institution that offers me a consistently positive atmosphere to learn new technologies and implement them for the betterment of the business.'

Person applying for manager's post

'To join a company that offers me a stable and positive atmosphere and inspires me to work efficiently for the betterment of all the stakeholders...'

Sales and customer care positions

'To join an organisation that offers me an environment for communicating and interacting with customers and other stakeholders...'

Career objectives can be anything and everything that a professional seeks. There is a good chance that the company will try to offer you whatever you have stated in the career objectives and then you would be stuck in a situation where you cannot handle what you desired. Every now and then, we come across people who are unhappy with their jobs.

The reasons of their unhappiness may vary—they do not like their work schedule, a colleague or their boss, etc. However, these vague reasons actually serve as a cover for the underlying dissatisfaction with the job that the employee is unaware of. It also happens if the employee has not given thought to his or her career goals and objectives. It is only when a person has clarity about his/her career goals and objectives that he or she gets satisfaction from his/her job and progress.

SAMPLE CAREER GOALS

Here is an illustrative list of some basic career goals that an employee should think about and keep in mind.

Growth In Resources

Change is the only constant, be it in everyday life or in a professional environment. With the change and growth in business, it is natural that one would have to constantly upgrade and enhance the knowledge and resources that he or she offers to the business or client. Therefore, upgrading one's knowledge and resources to grow as a professional is an important career goal that one should pursue.

Financial Aspect

Finance is one of the most important factors. If a person is underpaid, he or she will become bitter and frustrated and this will manifest in his or her work. If a person is overpaid, they may become lethargic and may not be as productive for the company as they were when they were hired and may soon be given the pink slip. Therefore, another important career goal is to pay only as much as the job position is worth for the company.

Satisfaction

Nothing in this world is done without a certain level of satisfaction being one of the primary requirements. An important career goal should be to be satisfied with whatever you are doing. Of course, that does not mean that you should stop experimenting or impede your enhancement process. You should make sure that you are completely satisfied with whatever job you are doing.

New Experiences

We spend almost three-fourths of our lives in the professional world. Therefore, it is logical that we try to progress and get ahead in our professional lives, but also to learn new things and gain new experiences. An added experience only enriches a person in terms of thought and knowledge. Therefore, accumulating experiences, such as learning about the cultures of different countries, meeting new people or becoming familiar with customs and traditions of another place/community, may also qualify as an important career goal. This will enable us to widen our perspective.

Stability

Another important thing that a person should look for is stability. Once a professional gets into a stable organisation, he or she does not bother about his/her day-to-day needs and can concentrate on growing as an individual and a professional, which will only add to the growth of the company.

CAREER STATEMENT

There are a few other important aspects of defining your career goals and objectives or having a career goal statement too. For example, you may define your long-term vision of a career—what would you like to achieve within a given time frame? You should set a time limit and check/assess your career statements.

Here are some examples of career statements.

Comprehensive Growth

Growth is the most important career goal that an employee should look at. There is never a limit to the growth of an individual in a job. In fact, even if a person becomes the CEO of a company, the next level of growth for the individual on a professional level is being an entrepreneur or becoming a proprietor. However, growth does not happen overnight, and diligence and dedication to a job are among the most important aspects of growth. Therefore, one should be dedicated and serious about the job. Only when a person achieves consistency, will he/she be able to achieve comprehensive growth on a professional level.

Management

Another example of a career goal is setting a time-frame for becoming a manager or a leader. Once you have mastered the art of meeting goals, you should seek a pathway for becoming a leader in your organisation.

Second Career

One of the most important advantages of having a second career is that a person becomes financially free and can, therefore, take certain risks in his or her job, which would otherwise not be possible. Risks are just opportunities in disguise and there is a chance that the risks may actually turn out to be lucrative prospects for the company that the individual is working for.

Logical Conclusion: A Business

After spending considerable years in a profession/ business, it is only logical for a person to think of having a business of their own. Once the person has a business of his or her own, he/she can use all the expertise and knowledge he/she has about the business for his/her own benefit. Therefore, ultimately having one's own business may also be one of the career goals.

Gaining Expertise

It goes without saying that once a person spends a certain length of time in a business or profession, he/she becomes experienced in the job. Once the individual's experience reaches a certain level, he/she is considered good enough to become a job consultant. Every employee should have a career goal to become so experienced in his/her profession that he/she can be hired as a consultant by other companies.

'People with clear, written goals accomplish far more in a shorter period of time than people without them could ever imagine.'
—Brian Tracy

Writing A CV

Don't let lack of work experience deter you from applying for a role where you otherwise meet most of the requirements. Instead, make the most of your other qualities: skills, attitude, potential and enthusiasm.

IDENTIFY WHAT QUALIFIES YOU FOR THE ROLE

It isn't only paid experience that counts. Voluntary or community work, coursework, work placements, personal projects and extra-curricular activities can all be highlighted to show your suitability. Think from the employer's perspective—decide on the most interesting factors where you have used relevant skills and then highlight these on your CV.

For instance, a graduate CV highlights education and training, including achievements and endorsements; emphasise 'project work' over 'work experience'. Breaking down each project into targets, result and learned competencies, shows the relevant skills and achievements in context.

MAKE YOURSELF IRRESISTIBLE
TO AN EMPLOYER

One of the hardest things to do convincingly on a CV is to convey desirable personality traits. Just writing that you are enthusiastic or motivated without giving supporting details isn't enough. Instead, demonstrate through examples.

Starting something from scratch and overcoming hurdles can show resourcefulness and determination. For instance: 'Launched a local skill-swapping service to slash household expenditure' or 'Found free advertising channels and enabled residents to make combined estimated savings of more than one lakh rupees in the first year'. You can use examples like these to illustrate important characteristics including the ability to get on with others or organisational and communication skills.

Working to help family finances or pay your way through college can reveal humility and strong ethics. 'Consistent work record; took up a variety of part-time jobs, since the age of sixteen, to contribute to education costs'. Learning about a role or sector through online communities, up-skilling through tutorials or conducting your own projects all show enthusiasm. These could fit into the education, training or skills section of your CV.

Graduate applicants can demonstrate these personality traits as well as attributes including numeracy and commercial awareness, which you could show through retail, marketing or sales work/assignments/opportunities.

Quantify achievements where possible (how much money saved, percentage of time reduced, etc.) and mention instances where you were promoted, rehired or given greater responsibility.

Speak The Same Language

This is especially the case for career changers, but all applicants should aim to use a language that an employer would expect to see from an ideal candidate. Include keywords throughout your CV—in job titles, skills and work summary. International finance and risk management etc., are keywords in their own right, and can be included in the skills section, titled 'specialised knowledge.'

Experiment With Layout

You don't need to always use a strict chronological work-history format or have the same section order. Put the most important information first—relevant project work can come before less relevant employment, while voluntary projects bridging your move into a new career could come before current work.

You can be flexible with the layout and include additional sections for work that is less relevant. You can also put your education before your work experience or extract relevant coursework and place that prominently.

Don't be tempted to flesh out a CV with long, rambling paragraphs and irrelevant details to compensate for a lack of work experience. Instead, write leanly and concisely, and focus on making it easy for your reader to find key information.

Consider putting a summary of points that stand out at the beginning of your CV. Put your name and contact details at the top of the page, then use the job title as a heading. Under this, summarise key details, such as duration of experience in a particular skill, project experience or summer placements, or a short branding statement highlighting your strengths and attributes. A couple of lines in note or bullet-point format (rather than entire sentences) can work well. Include a brief covering letter explaining your reasons for applying and your interest in the company.

Tailoring Your CV

KEEP CALM
AND
TAILOR YOUR CV

It is essential to tailor your CV for each role that you apply for.

- Read the job description
- Research the company
- Link both the points to your relevant skills and experience

For many job seekers, it's not uncommon to find twenty or so positions you'd like to apply for when conducting an online job search.

It may sound like a time-consuming process, but making the effort to tailor your CV to suit the requirements of each job that you are applying for can greatly increase your chances of securing an interview. These are the main areas of your CV that should be adapted to meet the exact requirements.

Personal Statement

You have read the requirements of the advertised position and understand what qualities the recruiter is looking for in a candidate. Sum up your unique selling points and, in a brief sentence, state your accomplishments and how these will help you succeed in the job you are applying for.

Employment History

If you are applying for a managerial position but have never previously worked as a manager, emphasise that your previous roles involved considerable responsibility and decision-making duties, such as delegation, chairing meetings, training staff, etc.

You may want to focus more on the innovative ways in which you have achieved success in the role to show your competency. Make it clear that whatever it is that they want, you will be able to fulfil their needs.

Skills

Perhaps most of the roles you desire to apply for will require a similar set of skills, but that doesn't mean you should leave out this section. Think how easy it would be for a recruiter to see that you're suitable if the skills you demonstrate are in the same order as listed in their job description.

Hobbies And Interests

Most job advertisements stipulate certain personality traits required for positions. So identify what they are and see how your hobbies can relate to the requirements.

If you are applying for a senior position, then the fact that you captained your football team and ran training sessions will demonstrate your leadership and organisational ability. If you are seeking a position as a designer, then mention the exhibitions that you attend or are actively involved in and names of the designers you admire.

If you want to position yourself as one of the strongest candidates for the job, it is worth doing your homework on the company that you are applying to. Their job advertisement will provide you with a glimpse of what the company is like, but you can find valuable information on their corporate website that will help you understand what they may be looking for in a job applicant. Try and align your CV with the company ethos.

Presentation And Layout

6

GETTING THE FORMAT RIGHT

Chronological CV	Skill-based CV
Starts with your most recent job, and then works backwards	Presents your main skills and key strengths
Advantages	**Advantages**
• Emphasises continuity and progression over time • Easy to follow • Works well if you have worked for well-known companies	• Strong emphasis on skills • Jobs and work history are secondary • Overcomes the difficulty of having too little or too much experience • Flexible
Disadvantages	**Disadvantages**
• It may not be a good choice if your career is patchy • It may not be a good option if you are changing your stream • It is not a good choice if you are new to the job market	• Difficult if you want to emphasise continuity • Might lose the impact of any prestigious companies you have worked for

It is imperative that the presentation and structure of your CV is excellent in order to give a good impression.

- Your CV should be clean and well laid out; leave appropriate white space to make it easier for the employer to read.
- It should be no longer than two pages unless your industry has its own standards, for instance, if you are expected to include your projects.
- Use professional fonts like Arial, 10pt. Avoid using italics; use bold text for headings only.
- Start each bullet point with a verb such as 'created', 'managed', 'increased' and 'improved', etc.

Spelling and punctuation must be perfect; after you have proofread and spell-checked your CV, give it to a friend to check it for readability and any errors that you may have missed.

Even the best-written CV in the world can be let down by a lack of proper presentation.

Although the content is undoubtedly of paramount importance, a CV has to be both well written and presented professionally in order to catch the recruiter's eye.

It is worth noting that when it comes to formatting, the approach may be industry-dependent. But there are a few simple rules which should generally be adhered to and, if implemented correctly, can dramatically increase your chances of success.

LAYOUT: DOS AND DON'TS

Dos

Keep it short and sweet: The most effective CVs aren't just informative, they're also concise. Try to get straight to the most pertinent points and ideally take up no more than two sides of an A4 page.

Choose a professional font: A professional font ensures that your CV can be easily read and scanned.

Remember: Comic Sans is not your friend.

Present things in a logical order: Use sufficient spacing, clear section headings (work experience or education) and a reverse chronological order to keep things clear and legible. Also highlight your most recent achievements.

Play up your strengths: Format your CV to maximise the impact of your application. For example, if you feel a lack of experience is holding you back, lead with education instead. As long as you can relate it back to the role in question, how you order the sections is up to you.

Use bullet points: They're a great way to draw attention to any key facts or relevant information, allowing a hiring manager to skim the document easily and see your significant achievements.

Other things to do: Include contact details; keep email address professional; maintain consistent formatting; ask someone to check your CV.

Don'ts

Be afraid of white space: Don't fear the gaps. Even if you think your CV looks quite bare, as long as you've included all the relevant information and applicable, quantifiable achievements, you needn't worry.

Remember: Sometimes less is more.

Try to include too much: The ideal CV should be a checklist of all your accomplishments. It should not be your life story. Tailoring your CV to the role is a great way to skim some of the fat and keep waffle to a minimum.

Include irrelevant information: Before including any points in your application, ask yourself: 'Will it help me get the role?' If the answer is 'No', take it out. Hobbies and interests are a great example. If they don't help you stand out, don't waste valuable space.

Don't forget the cover letter: Although it is often seen as a different entity altogether, your cover letter is attached to your CV and both are vital in helping you clinch the right role. If it is utilised properly, your CV becomes the perfect document to reinforce your talent. Even if the recruiter did not ask for it, include one. Every extra opportunity to sell yourself should be taken.

Experimenting with the length: You may think that changing font size is a great way to fit your CV into two pages. But whether you're using a large font to make your application seem longer or you're using smaller font to make sure everything fits, you're not fooling anyone. Also, check the spacing of margins.

Other things not to do: Use crazy colours and fonts, and include unnecessary references or a selfie.

CV HEADINGS

Your CV's heading is the first thing that prospective employers will see when they look at it. It's their first impression of you; it is absolutely vital that you present it in the best format possible.

Do not start your CV with any of these.

Curriculum Vitae	☒
Confidential	☒
CV	☒

'Confidential' as a heading is not a good idea because a CV by its very nature will contain some confidential or personal information. Besides, employers neither do, nor have the time for passing around your CV to others unless it is part of the recruitment and candidate selection process.

Your name may be a good heading for your CV.

Writing a CV heading

Font size: 20 points	☑
Boldface	☑
Centred on the page	☑

CV heading tips

Tip 1: Do not capitalise the CV heading as it gives the impression that you're shouting and it is also more difficult to read.

Tip 2: Give the name that you are generally known by rather than your full legal name.

Tip 3: Do not use nicknames, for instance, Raj instead of Rajkumar; it makes you look less professional.

Basic CV Structure

7

DETAILS TO BE INCLUDED IN A CV

Contact Details

Make sure to use the phone number and email address that you use most often. You don't want to miss an opportunity by failing to respond to their call to an interview in a timely fashion.

Nationality And Passport Details

This is relevant only if you are applying for a job overseas.

Personal Summary

Ensure that there is a 'Summary of experience' section at the top of your CV, which includes relevant experience.

Skills Summary

Your recruiter/employer may not have more than a few seconds to read your CV, so including a skills section can capture their attention by making it clear what you can offer. Use a brief bulleted list of the skills and experience that you possess that are relevant to the role, such as the software you have worked with.

Wherever possible, use the same adjectives as those used in the advertisement. For example, if the ad has the words 'effective administrative abilities and excellent interpersonal skills', these should be mentioned under the skills section in the same order, although not verbatim.

Work Experience

Talking about your business or project successes will help you to showcase your skills and experience. This is your work history and includes any relevant voluntary work experience. Work backwards from your most recent job and don't leave any gaps; if you took a year off, undertook out an interim assignment or travelled for six months, say so.

If you are a graduate, you may not have a great deal of work experience. In that case, highlight the relevant skills that you gained in your course or through voluntary work experience. Again, list each position in reverse order, so that the most recent appears first.

Education And Training

If you have an advanced degree, few people are going to be concerned about your school final results. Be sure to include any training courses that you have done, which are relevant to the job that you are applying for.

Hobbies

Although optional, do include a section on hobbies and interests, but keep it brief.

References

Actual references are rarely included in CVs. It is usually fine to simply say 'References are available on request.'

FINAL CHECKS

Don't forget to spell-check! Remember, it is the first impression your potential employer will have of you, so take the time to get it right. Double-check layout or typing errors.

The perfect CV is the CV that achieves an interview; no more, no less. When the CV puts your name on the interview shortlist, it has done its job.

Make It Special

MAKE YOUR CV UNIQUE AND SPECIAL

Here are a few guidelines rather than ground rules; nothing is inscribed in stone!

There are only ideas and concepts which have been proven in the job market by thousands of job hunters. You will receive as many different bits of advice regarding your CV as the number of people you show it to. Before you take an advice, ask yourself the 'quality control' question.

The CV is a door opener. It is not only the first thing the potential employer sees about you; more significantly it is the only part of the entire job selection process on which you as a job seeker have 100 per cent control. You can't control the availability of the sort of job you want, you can't control who gets shortlisted. You can only control how you project yourself in your CV.

Your CV won't win you the job because it is rare for anyone to get hired on the strength of their CV alone, but your CV will get you the ticket to the job race. Your CV is the ticket to the candidacy, so it goes without saying that it should be letter perfect, neat, easy to read and well organised.

From the outset, from the stage of selection, the recruiter is looking for reasons to turn you down and not to take you on! Advertisements these days attract hundreds of applicants, sometimes thousands of them. Thus, the your CV should shine and make a style statement.

As a recruiter, if there is a pile of CVs, the main task is to reduce the mountain of 'job hopefuls' to a molehill of 'possible jobs'. The maxim 'When in doubt, throw it out!' is very often used by recruiters.

The recruiter always thinks that he or she is good at their job simply because it never emerges how good the person whose CV has just been rejected might have been. Recruiters never gain any negative information about potentially brilliant candidates they have passed over at the shortlisting stage. So right from the very start, your CV has to be special. State in as many ways as possible: 'See me, see me'.

In an ideal world, a CV should be specifically written and customised for each job, but today's job market requires you to send off numerous CVs to potential employers because competition is fierce and quality opportunities are scarce.

As a job hunter, one needs two basic CVs.

- A CV built around your present job
- A CV aimed at the next job in your career

Make sure you remember which CV you have sent to which employer. It sounds easy enough, but a lot of applicants get it wrong. Some careful administration is needed here.

As with most things in life, there are no absolutes and CVs are no exception. There are things which work in the job market and things which do not. Here are some practical tips and ideas which have justified their inclusion through trial and error in the job market.

The CV serves three basic requirements.

- To highlight your value to a potential employer

- To provide a structure and a curriculum for the interview

- To act as a record of the substance of the interview

Writing a CV is not difficult but if it is to achieve its purpose, it will require time, effort, reflection, creativity and determination.

Above all, the CV must be written with the potential employer firmly in mind. Authors write with their readers in mind, advertisers with their potential customers in mind, and so must you. You are selling your skills and experience in the job market and you must ensure that your personal brochure presents you in the best possible way to your potential buyer.

Remember: All these things are incorrectly inferred from a spelling or typing mistake.

- You cannot spell
- You are lazy
- You are inattentive to detail
- You are not capable of representing the company
- You do not really want the job

There will be enough reasons for the recruiter to put you in the 'No' pile without you providing for it by spelling errors or typos. It is not enough to run the CV through spell check. This will catch the spelling errors but not the 'typos' and a typo will have the same effect on a selector as a spelling error.

Make your CV easy to read. Use short sentences. Long sentences are complicated. Short sentences can be skimmed quickly. Short sentences have power. The active tense is the best. Unless you are going for a job as a writer, facts are more important than style. The tabloid press approach is the best. Remember, you only have sixty seconds to get your message across.

Certain words are far more positive in their impact than others of roughly the same meaning. Once the CV has been written, every word needs to be examined carefully to see whether another more powerful or positive equivalent can be used.

Generally speaking, the weaker words occur when the job holder is either passive or reactive to the work situation rather than in control of things.

Here are some examples.

maintained	prevented	rejected
ordered	provided	revamped
performed	recommended	specified
prepared	rectified	supported

There is nothing intrinsically wrong with these words, but they give the impression of a passive person, someone who responds to situations rather than initiating them. With a little more thought and research, more positive synonyms can be found and used to create a completely different impression—it is not what you present but rather the way you present it!

Remember, you do not have to tell the selector everything. One of the reasons that CVs fail is because they say too much; because the more you say, the more you will entrap yourself. In terms of a CV, if you write more, the selector may find more reasons to turn you down. So keep it brief.

How brief is brief? Well, some say, if you say it all in two or three pages at the most, there must be something wrong. There are many advisers who would say that one page is all it should take. Some are of the opinion that the more senior you are, the shorter your CV can be. There are no absolutes, but a reasonable rule of thumb is minimum one or two pages and a maximum of four pages, including a technical page if applicable.

The CV is often used to provide a structure to the job interview. This purpose is frequently ignored or unappreciated by the job seeker. If you tell an employer that you failed one of your examinations, then the employer will talk about your failure. It is in your interest to include only positive information and not feed the interviewer with negative points. Stay positive.

Put information about your age on the back page. I would suggest you consider doing this anyway, since there are few jobs in which your age is more significant than your academic qualifications or what you do.

Your CV should be user friendly, easy to work with. For example, if you have a higher qualification, then please don't tell them that you first went to a good school. Make yourself easy to work with by starting with your highest qualification first and going backwards.

What often happens is that on leaving college, many people prepare a CV for the first time. From then on, when the person wishes to change jobs, their current employment information is tacked on to the college CV and it grows and grows. Each time you make a trip into today's highly competitive job market, make a fresh CV.

THE REVERSE CHRONOLOGY RULE

'Where are the skills and abilities I am currently selling— in my current job or in the one I took when I left school?' The most recent experience is the most relevant to job hunt. So use this by employing the reverse chronological rule when writing about career and achievements. Doesn't career sound better than 'experience' or 'work', and the heading 'Career and Achievements to Date' even better imply that: 'this is what I've done so far, but I still have much to do.'

Everybody has 'experience' but it sounds uninteresting on a CV. Achievements are far more powerful.

Layout: Framed

Sometimes CVs give the impression that they have been block heads. The content could be excellent but the visual presentation may be awful. Make it look attractive. If you look at a picture which has been framed, the margin at the bottom of the picture is usually larger than the one at the top or the sides.

The back pages of CVs are frequently only partially filled. This is a waste of an opportunity to either add relevant information or spread your information so that it looks more attractive. Half close your eyes and look at your CV. Does the block of information look lopsided? Play about with the layout so that you gain a centrally balanced picture.

Use quality paper. Avoid cheap photocopying paper.

Employers are mainly interested in the relevance of your skills, experience and, more importantly, your attitude, commitment and motivation. Consequently, if you feel bound to mention references, then the simple statement, 'References are available on request' should suffice.

After you have completed your CV, a useful discipline is to write your ideal reference. What would you like your previous boss to say about you? How can you justify all the points you made about your work and your approach to it? Once you have done this, telephone your potential referees and bring them up to date with your career aspirations, plans and actions. This is particularly important when you want to change your career; it is important to emphasise those aspects of your job and skills that are allied to your new sphere of aspirations.

If a photograph is called for, go to a professional portrait photographer and tell him or her exactly what you want. Refer to pictures from business journals or company corporate literature that you like and brief the photographer on the image you wish to project. Sometimes it is helpful to decide on a set of three adjectives—competent, dynamic and hardworking; professional, thorough and reliable; creative, enthusiastic and dynamic—to describe the image you feel you have or wish to project, and tell the photographer about it.

Ask to be photographed in a half-smile. People looking at photographs of individuals with a half-smile rate them as more intelligent, friendly and better with interpersonal skills—the sort of things you would want in an employee anyway.

If you normally wear glasses, wear them for the photograph.

According to experts, coloured clothes make a person look more powerful. The point here, of course, is that you should think carefully about what you wear and the image or expectations it will create.

However, the basic rule is: don't include a photograph unless you have to and if you must send a photograph, try getting it right.

Salary

The iron rule of wages says that employers will pay you as little as they can to get you, motivate you and prevent you from leaving. Salary, then, is a negotiation point. The second rule of negotiation is 'only negotiate from power' (the first being only negotiate with decision-makers). When you are one of 150, you have no power. So then is not the time to mention salary or what you want.

When you get on the shortlist you are one of perhaps five people but this is still not the time to mention pay and conditions. Now, supposing you are the last candidate in the ring, do you have power?

Always, always, always leave salary negotiation for as late as possible in the selection process. The little 'c' before the salary section in an advertisement for a job stands for 'circa' and in salary terms that can mean as much as 10 per cent higher or 10 per cent below. Remember, if you start on a low salary with a firm, you will stay low. One of the reasons for changing jobs is to improve your financial situation, so employers expect you to negotiate.

Sending your CV to agencies and headhunters, however, is different. These firms are paid a commission (sometimes as high as 35 per cent) of the first year's earnings. They have a vested interest in getting as much for your 'head' as possible. In the salary stakes, they are going to be on your side, so provide them with the details of your current package and, of course, what you would like to earn. You will get the benefit of some realistic feedback on your market worth.

Letting agencies know how much you earn and how much you expect (or will move for) does not preclude salary negotiations with your employer.

Career Summary

Constructing a career summary is perhaps the most important and significant preparation for the CV. Whether or not you decide to use a career summary in your final CV, it is still a very useful discipline. A career summary is a simple statement of twenty or so words that encapsulates your career aspirations and what you wish to sell in the market. Imagine that you have only thirty or so words to convince a prospective employer to listen to what you have to say. This process will help the reader to focus on what exactly it is that you want to say.

The summary brings three potential benefits.

- First, it will help you become clear on which of your skills you wish to utilise and the kind of career or job you want.

- Second, when placed strategically after your name, address and telephone number, it will act like a banner headline for your CV. It acts as a preconditioning statement, that is, it conditions the reader to anticipate positive information about you.

- Third, a career statement can be used rather like a go/no-go gauge in quality control. Everything that you wish to put on your CV should in some way support and justify the career statement. If you wish to include something about yourself which does not match the criteria of your career summary, then it may be wise to censor the item.

SAKE

SAKE stands for the four attributes of candidates in which a prospective employer has an interest, namely your:

- skills,
- attitude,
- knowledge and
- experience.

Here is the procedure of writing a career summary.

- Take a sheet of A4 paper and put your name in a circle in the centre and then, from the circle, make four arrows pointing at skills, attitude, knowledge and experience.

- Now, in terms of these areas, write what you have, what you are, what you have done and what you can offer. Let your imagination ebb and flow, jotting down anything and everything that comes to mind.

You can show your mind map to your partner, to a friend or colleague whose views you value, because we sometimes miss the obvious or even devalue what we have to offer.

- Next, go through the mind map, first taking out all the things you don't want to use. Having done this, rank in order all those aspects that a potential employer would be interested in. This will give you the curriculum for your career summary.

- Write your career summary in the third person singular as if you were an employment agency sending out details about yourself to a potential employer.

- Revise your career statement until you feel comfortable with it.

Achievements, Not Just Responsibilities

People are sometimes too lazy to write their own CVs and they end up writing all their responsibilities. You should remember that when personnel departments write job descriptions, they are doing so for pay grading and appraisal assessment, not for an individual to get a job elsewhere. Who in their right mind would want a CV that includes information written by someone else? It is like trying to sell a product using the raw material procurement specifications and not developing any sales literature.

When you write about your job, don't say what someone else asked you to do based upon your job description but say what you actually did and how good you were at it.

Achievements are FAB

There is a very simple process for writing your achievements. It is called FAB—F for 'Feature', A for 'Analysis' and B for 'Benefit'.

F for Feature: First of all, list all the things that you have actually done in a job. All those special successes, the times when you thought to yourself, 'I really did well there' or 'I really earned my salary there'. These are the highlights of your job.

A for Analysis: Now, we must work on the 'A'—Analysis. We must analyse the feature. What was it, how big was it, who was involved, what were the savings to the company? Ask yourself the question, 'Is there any way I can get a number attached to the feature? Is there anyway of quantifying an achievement? If an achievement has a percentage or anything that can be measured?' Reasons for a number attached to it, looks more impressive, more credible and more understandable.

B for Benefit: Let's now deal with the 'B'. This comes straight from an established sales technique which suggests that people don't buy features but they do buy its benefits. In other words, we want the benefits brought by the features, not the features themselves!

Use The Past For The Future

Wherever possible, use the immediate past tense form of the verb to introduce an achievement. The noun form or the participle form is not as powerful.

Here are some examples.

'Managed' rather than 'the management', 'improved' rather than 'the improvement', 'investigated' rather than 'the investigation', that is, the past tense rather than the noun. And use 'designed' rather than 'designing', 'analysed' rather than 'analysing', 'directed' rather than 'directing', that is, the past tense rather than the participle. The past tense gives the impression that you have actually done something. It is completed, finished and achieved, which in a CV is the impression you want to create.

Deleting the first person, 'I', will make it easier for you to give yourself proper credit without appearing over-boastful.

When using the past tense, you don't have to keep using 'I'; you can replace it with an asterisk or star. The second point is that you can now indent your achievements on the page so that they stand out better and the eye of the reader is drawn towards them.

Tell Them What They Want To Know

The next important principle is to include only relevant information. If something does not support your career goal, then think before including it.

Reasons For Leaving

It is better not to include reasons for leaving on your CV. Such information can only serve to remind the potential employer that you are in control of your career rather than vice versa. Also, there are basically only four reasons why people leave jobs—better prospects, more pay, relocation or they were fired. Any of them, if the employer thinks about them seriously, makes you a potential risk as an employee—the question 'Will you stay?' is raised by the first three and the last will guarantee you stay unemployed. It is better to explain such things during the interview than to try to justify your career moves at the CV stage.

RECENT JOBS ONLY

Most employers are mainly interested in what you have been doing recently. What you did ten years ago is unlikely to make a significant contribution to your next job. Sometimes a previous job is directly useful and then it should be included. You will have to decide for yourself how best to account for the early years of your career on your CV. The basic question to ask is: Does it fit or support my present career aspirations? If it does not help you in any way, then it should be omitted.

Education

Your education successes should be set out on the same principles as in the career section. Thus, the reverse chronological rule applies just as much to education as it does to your career.

In the same way, your qualification is more important than where it was gained, which is more important, again, than when it was achieved.

NO GIMMICKS

Do not be tempted to use gimmicks. If your CV needs a special gimmick to gain attention, rather than your achievements or skills, then your CV may get noticed but it will not pass further scrutiny.

What to leave out?

As the CV will form the basis of the interview, and negative information at the interview always attracts more supplementary and probing questions, your CV should contain only that which is positive.

SUGGESTED OMISSIONS

Here are some things you might consider omitting.

- Examinations you have failed due to health reasons
- Major illness, both physical and mental
- Junior jobs irrelevant to your present career thrust
- Employment of less than a year
- Reason for leaving employment
- Dates of qualifications
- Political affiliations
- Your current salary and benefits
- Your anticipated salary and benefits
- Addresses of the firms you have worked for
- Names or job titles of the people you worked for
- Do not use 'I' until really necessary
- Do not use jargon
- Do not use abbreviations that will not be understood by all the potential recipients of your CV
- Do not make spelling or grammatical errors
- Do not use photocopies
- Do not use cheap paper

- Do not use extreme typefaces, silly visual effects or a brochure format
- Do not include a photograph

COVERING LETTER

The covering letter is the packaging for the CV. If the letter does not command the attention of the selector, then why should he or she go on to read the CV?

Here are some obvious basics.

First, where possible the covering letter should be typed. Most written business communication is typed; if your letter is not, you are signalling quite clearly to your future employer that you are an outsider trying to get in.

Of course, spelling and grammar should be correct. Split infinitives annoy people. You must remember that at this stage in the selection process, it is only your letter and CV that contain information about you, and who wants an employee who cannot even present himself or herself correctly?

Structure Of The Covering Letter

The purpose of the covering letter is very simple—to get the recipient to read your CV—no more, no less. Although this is obvious and simple, it is surprising how many covering letters:

- are too long.
- repeat the content of the CV.
- are written from the applicant's point of view.

- contain negative information and besides all this, contain spelling and grammatical errors.

The covering letter needs only three paragraphs.

First paragraph: Give your reason for writing. A good way of ensuring this is to use the sales letter strategy of beginning this paragraph with the word 'Your'.

For example:

- Your advertisement was of great interest...
- Your company enjoys an excellent reputation in engineering...
- Your article in *Business Week...*

Employers are bound to be interested in what is happening from their viewpoint.

Second paragraph: Customise your CV and direct the reader to some unique selling point which meets a specific need of the prospective employer.

For example:

- You will see from my enclosed CV...
- Customer services has been the thrust of my career...

Third paragraph: This is to ask for the interview, although interviews are work for personnel people. So we translate this into 'discussion' or 'meeting'.

For example:

- The opportunity for a discussion...
- The chance to meet you...

The third paragraph is to prompt the reader into some form of action. For example:

- I look forward to hearing from you…

If you are applying for jobs, where some degree of confidence and assertiveness is required or expected, you may say:

- Perhaps, I may telephone your office next week to see how you would wish to progress further in the matter...

Dos And Don'ts

DOs

- Construct your CV with your prospective employer in mind. Look at the job advertisement or specifications and think about what the job involves and what the employer needs. Find out about the main activities of the employer.

- Tailor your CV to suit the job requirements. Your CV shouldn't be your life story but should be tailored keeping in mind the job you're applying for, focusing on the parts that are important for that particular job. No one wants to read a CV that is squashed together and includes too much information.

- Make your CV clear, neat and tidy. Get somebody to check your spelling and grammar. Your CV should be easy to read with sufficient space between each section and plenty of white space. Use left-justified text as it's easier to read, using black text on good quality white or cream paper.

- View your experience in a positive light. Try to look objectively at your experiences (even the bad ones) and identify what you learned or what skills you developed in the process. This is the picture you should present to the employer.

- Place the important information upfront. Put experience and education achievements in reverse chronological order.

- Include experience and interests that might be of use to the employer: IT skills, voluntary work, foreign language competency, driving skills and leisure interests that demonstrate teamworking/organisation/leadership skills.

- Put your name and email address on every page—in case the pages of your CV get separated.

- Use positive language. When describing your work achievements, use power words such as 'launched', 'managed', 'coordinated', 'motivated', 'supervised' and 'achieved'.

- Quote concrete outcomes to support your claims. For example, 'This reduced the development time from seven to three days' or 'This revolutionised the company's internal structure...'

- Make use of the internet for sample CVs and CV templates to help maximise the impact of your CV and to get ideas for layout and tone.

DON'Ts

- Include information which may be viewed negatively, such as failed exams, divorces, failed business ventures, reasons for leaving a job, points on your driving license. Don't lie, but just don't include this kind of information. Don't give the interviewer any reason to eliminate you at this stage.

- Include anything that might discriminate against you, such as date of birth, marital status, race, gender or disability.

- Include salary information and expectations. Leave this for negotiations after your interview, when the employers are convinced that they want to employ you.

- Make your CV more than two pages long. You can make space by excluding or editing information that is less important. For example, you do not need to include referees; just state they are available on request. Don't include all the jobs you have had since school, mention just the relevant ones. Add details about your most recent qualifications, which are more relevant, but summarise the rest.

- Dilute your important messages. Don't bother with a list of schools you attended with grades and addresses, don't include a long list of hobbies or a long work history. Concentrate on demonstrating the skills they need, your achievements and what benefits your clients have gained from your work.

- Use jargon, acronyms, technical terms, unless essential.

- Lie; employers have ways of checking what you wrote is true or not, and may sack you if they take you on and find out you've lied to them.

WRITING A CV

Make your CV visually appealing. Look at how others have done their CVs. Ask your professors and colleagues for examples. Start your CV with general contact information that includes your name, address, telephone, fax, email and URL (if you have a web page about yourself as a professional). Include these sections in your CV: Contact information, education and experience. Include these sections depending on your strengths and interests: honours and awards (from post-secondary school), teaching and research interests, publications, professional activities (committee memberships, intern experience, relevant voluntary work), skills (second language and/or computer proficiencies), and references (you may include these or indicate they are 'available on request'). Check your CV carefully for spelling and typographical errors. Use formatting, such as bullets, italics or bold font, only sparingly and use beige, white or a neutral colour paper that weighs between 20–50 gsm.

Don't try to do it all by yourself the first time. Seek help from others, such as faculty advisors, career specialists or colleagues. The CV should be a formal document and should include important data. Don't include the following information: age, ethnic identity, political affiliation, religious preferences, hobbies, marital status, sexual orientation, place of birth, photographs, height, weight and health status. Don't pad your CV with excessive information about research or teaching. Instead, provide the titles of research projects and course names along with brief summaries of your work. Don't include information that is humorous.

Digital CV

CVs are now more likely to be sent digitally—some employers use software to sift through applications—but presentation and delivery aren't the only aspects that have changed.

Social media and other forms of modern communication are more visual than ever before. And since your résumé is your number one communication tool in the job application process, why shouldn't that be highly visual, too?

Mapping out your educational background, work experience and skill set in a crisp, aesthetically pleasing way is the best way to compel a hiring manager to want to learn more about you.

DIGITAL TOOLS

- **Put it together:** Import your profile data from LinkedIn and Facebook, and ResumUP; craft a gorgeous infographic complete with your work history, skills, achievements, key values and even your personality type. Share it with potential employers in PDF or PNG form. This is pretty affordable.

- **Visualise me:** 'Visualise me' auto-transforms your professional accomplishments into a simple yet compelling data using the data from your LinkedIn profile. Choose from six style themes and dozens of fonts and colour schemes for your digital résumé.

- **My stats:** A cool 'My Stats' section lets you highlight numbers—like years of experience in a certain industry or number of press impressions you secured for a client. Download the infographic as a PDF or PNG or share it as a link. It's totally free and awesome.

- **Kukook:** This site provides at least twenty impressive, easy-to-edit résumé templates that are modern, clean and supremely polished. They open in Microsoft Word for straight-forward plug-and-play. Just customise with your personal information, save (all résumé templates come with DOC and PDF file types) and send off.

- **Creddle:** Creddle is a completely free résumé-making site that tailor-makes an auto-formatted document from your personal information (enter manually or sync from LinkedIn). Select one template, then change headers, add colour and move sections, at will.

Once you're done, you can share it online, embed it on your personal website or send it as a PDF or DOCX file. You can even use *Creddle* to quickly create a cover letter with a nameplate and contact links that match your résumé.

Note: The free version includes three résumé designs and basic analytics (how many times your online résumé has been viewed and from what sources).

Caveat: Don't sacrifice clarity and coherence for visual glitter. No matter how much your résumé pops, if the hiring manager can't glance through it and get a clear sense of who you are and what you have to offer, you're not any closer to that offer letter.

Online CV

Recruiters and hiring managers are increasingly sourcing (and checking) candidates online. The report *What employers look up on social media sites* found that employers are interested in previous work history, recommendations and information such as personal interests.

Improve your chances by providing this information online.

LINKEDIN PROFILE

On LinkedIn, you only have one version, so it must appeal to different readers (recruiters, peers and employers) and be tailored for both networking and job searching. Don't just copy and paste your paper CV, but give a bigger picture of your strengths, interests and professional activity.

LinkedIn profiles are far more dynamic than traditional CVs. Various applications let you add blogposts, a portfolio and presentations and upload files (such as your CV). Keep your profile active with status updates and tweets. Highlight your professional reputation through adding recommendations and connections, and joining relevant groups. Include a professional photo and feel free to add personal interests.

Treat your profile as a networking tool to your boss. Build your profile, connecting with people you know.

While traditional CVs are concise, your LinkedIn profile can contain paragraphs and full sentences. Using the first-person (as in 'I specialise in' rather than 'Specialist in') adds a more personal tone.

If you're job hunting, optimise your profile with keywords— job titles, areas of expertise and terms typically found in your target job descriptions. The special section of your summary is ideal for listing your professional skills.

OTHER PROFILES AND CVS

Google Profile

Use your Google account to create a profile: upload a photo, add links (such as the link to your LinkedIn profile) and write a page that serves as a CV, including a short introduction, your current occupation, employment history and so on.

A Profile on both LinkedIn and Google rates high when your name is Googled, helping to overlook any negative information about you.

Facebook CV

A creative idea from JobMob which uses the new home page layout (with your profile photo on the left and five tagged photos across the top) as CV sections.

Twitter CV

Upload your CV to display as your Twitter background with *www.twitres.com*.

Visual CV

Embed audio, video, graphs and PowerPoint files on your own page. You can then send the link to contacts, potential employers and so on.

Video CV

Not appropriate for all sectors, but if done professionally, a video presentation can get results. You can create a webcam clip, hosting it with your CV, on a site such as *Meet the Real Me*. But even a brief clip uploaded on YouTube can help with remote networking or a job search. Send the link in a speculative email, if you're currently unavailable to meet in person. Make the clip interesting. Don't read out your CV or use bland clichés. Be specific about what you offer the company or tell a relevant story to exemplify a strength or personal quality.

TIPS ON ONLINE CV

Recruitment is well and truly entrenched in the online world now, meaning that it's becoming increasingly important to make sure your online CV is up to scratch. While online CVs share many of the same virtues of the traditional paper format, there are a few subtle differences that you should consider before penning your résumé and uploading it on the web.

Dos

- Ensure that you list all your qualifications, achievements and any other courses or certifications that you may have undertaken.

- If possible, try to back this up with actual achievements that you feel are appropriate.

- Try and include company names—as this will serve to shore up your CV and reassure employers that they can check with the companies for references.

- Be sure to highlight clearly any unique or extra special piece of information about you and your career. This is what can attract an employer and will stick in his or her mind when it comes to calling you for an interview.

Don'ts

- Lie or exaggerate about any part of your career. The internet makes it so much easier for companies to scout around and carry out a background check, meaning you will be found out should you tell any white lies. This will do your prospects of securing an interview no good at all.

- Include too many personal contact details. Remember you are still sending a great deal of information about yourself to someone you don't know. Try and stick to one point of contact such as email or telephone rather than offering several options.

- Finally, avoid 'building up' your CV too much because, chances are employers will be able to tell if you're lying, especially in the age of online recruitment where it's much easier to find out information about people.

PHRASES TO AVOID ON A CV—VIDEO ADVICE

There are certain clichés that need to be avoided at all costs. Not only do they take up valuable space on your CV, but they also don't help recruiters in understanding the 'real you'. Acting as your personal advertisement, your CV enables buyers (employers) to see what you can offer and so the presentation and structure of your CV is crucial. Unfortunately, too many people follow the tradition of using stock phrases and 'key' words that they think will help them stand out from the crowd. Due to this overuse, many recruiters have become immune to certain phrases.

Not making your CV stand out from the crowd can seriously damage your job search chances.

Here are the most common phrases and some suggested alternatives.

- **Team player:** As it's unlikely that anyone would claim the opposite, statements like this become meaningless. The most effective way to get your future employer's attention is to demonstrate your experience by giving a real-life example, for instance, explaining your role when you worked within a team to achieve a specific goal.

- **Project management skills:** This is just a fancy way of saying that you are organised. Employers want to know what you have done in your current job that demonstrates your abilities. Have you organised an event or managed a budget? If so, tell them.

- **Result oriented:** Employers run businesses and they want a return on their investment in you. Convey and quantify your accomplishments and your potential to solve your future employer's problems. Did you increase sales? If so, by how much? Did you save money for your organisation? Did you achieve your targets in the face of difficult circumstances?

- **People management skills:** Does that mean that you were a manager or simply that you got on well with your customers and colleagues? 'Management' implies that you held a position of responsibility over other staff and can confuse employers. So, opt for words such as 'supervised' or 'coordinated' instead.

- **Responsible:** Everybody is responsible for something in their job. And, just because you are responsible for something does not necessarily make you a responsible person. Did you take on duties that were not part of your job specifics? Did you train staff or suggest/introduce a new initiative? Did you rescue a failing project and turn it around?

When writing your CV, bear in mind the role that you are applying for and tailor it accordingly by focusing on providing evidence relevant to the position.

By using examples of past experience, you will put yourself in a stronger position and stand out from your peers. So, drop the jargon and clichés and get personal.

Writing a winning CV can be a challenge, but by putting in the mileage you will have a document that will make employers take action and invite you for an interview. Then, the real selling begins!

Key Skills That
All CVs Need

Key Skills

CV Review

Technical Skills

- Outlook
- Word
- Excel
- PowerPoint
- Access

Memberships

- Chartered Financial Analyst (CFA)

Add some context

- These skills would read better with a brief description
  - **Excel**: Producing financial models and forecasts, etc.
- This section need not be application/tool specific, for instance, structuring capital through bonds and leveraged finance etc.

Memberships/Affiliations

- Must be industry specific (CFA and MBA etc.)

A CV ought to demonstrate all your skills. Ideally, you will be able to link your key skills to workplace experience, but if this is not possible, then try to cite ways in which you have used them outside of employment situations.

Most key skills fall into one of three categories.

TRANSFERABLE SKILLS

These are skills that have been acquired in one setting but can be used in many different sorts of businesses.

Everyone has transferable skills even if they don't recognise them. Sometimes, your current employer won't make it obvious that the skills you have acquired with them are transferable because they don't necessarily want you to realise how employable you are elsewhere.

Transferable Skills That You May Possess

- **Reading- or writing-related skills:** This means being able to digest written information and present it in written form as well.

- **Computer skills:** If you have an aptitude with computers and common office programmes, then consider this to be a transferable skill.

- **Management experience:** If you have managed people before, then you could transfer this experience to benefit another employer.

- **Commercial skills:** People who can negotiate and handle figures like turnover and gross profit often possess the sort of business acumen which is sought by many organisations.

- **Deadline success:** Being able to work to deadlines is something that doesn't happen in all jobs, but if you are used to it, then this is a key transferable skill desired in many companies.

JOB-RELATED SKILLS

These skills are specific to a certain line of employment or trade and may require you to have received training to perform.

More specific than transferable skills, job-related skills can get you work with another employer, who needs them. Despite this, transferable skills won't necessarily be of use to employers outside of the sector you already work in.

Here are a few examples of job-related skills.

- **Nursing skills:** Being a qualified nurse shows you have certain transferable skills like being caring or organised, but nursing itself is a job-related skill which only really works in the healthcare sector.

- **Mechanical engineering:** Being able to repair engines is a job-related skill. It may mean you can transfer into related sectors but probably only within similar roles unless you have other transferable skills to offer.

- **Accountancy qualifications:** Bookkeeping and accountancy roles are required in a wide range of organisations, which present plenty of job choices. However, such job-related skills narrow down the choice to certain types of jobs only.

ADAPTIVE SKILLS

These aptitudes are sometimes less obvious and harder to quantify because they rely on personality traits rather than learning.

Adaptive skills are ideal for CV personal statements or even a cover letter and can also be listed in your work experience if you prefer. Think about the sort of personality you have when discussing your adaptive skills. Some of the key ones to look out for are these.

- **Teamworking:** Not everyone is a team player, but teamworking is an important adaptive skill that many employers are looking for.

- **Loyalty:** Been in a job for a long time and seen it through thick and thin? This is an adaptive skill to mention on your CV.

- **Positivity:** If you are the sort of person who sees the glass as half full and not half empty, then this shows your positivity. Employers tend to favour positive people so mention this as an adaptive skill.

- **Creativity:** Some jobs cry out for creative people. If you paint, play music or are even good at telling jokes, then this may reflect your creative skills.

- **Adaptability:** This is something we all need in the workplace from time to time, but some are better at it than others so don't discount your adaptability as a skill.

- **Tenacity:** Taking ownership of problems and seeing them through is a key skill in many organisations. If you can demonstrate this from your past jobs, then include it on your CV.

Although adaptive skills may seem like the least important ones to mention because they are not specific to the job you are applying for, they can often mark you out from another candidate. Don't overlook the importance of your blend of adaptive skills which is as unique as you are.

Be proud of the skills that you have and see each of them as a way to progress in your career.

WHAT MAKES A CV STAND OUT?

Maximise Readability

It is essential for your CV to be easy for the reader to scan quickly and effectively. You need to separate different sections and insert clear section headings. Avoid long paragraphs; use bullet points to break up text into more manageable 'bite-size' chunks. It should be eye-catching and uncluttered. Check vigilantly for spelling and grammatical errors.

Include A Professional Profile And Objective

These sections should summarise and emphasise your key attributes and your intended future career path. Your words must flow seamlessly—avoid clichés and hyperbole. They should each be only a few lines in length but they must spark the reader's interest. If you can't successfully 'pitch' yourself in under ten lines, then you risk losing the reader's attention. Be brief—you can highlight examples in later sections, but be persuasive.

Include Achievements Where Possible

If you can include an 'achievements' section, then it can make an instant and dramatic difference to the power of your CV, enabling you to distinguish yourself from other candidates. This is no time for false modesty. Utilise the space allocated to highlight where you have excelled and how you plan to attain similar results in the future endeavours.

Keep Your CV Concise And To The Point

Your CV should be informative, but concise. In general, two A4 pages is the maximum. Only include information which will actually help to sell you. Recruiters don't want to waste time reading details irrelevant to your ability.

Tailor Your CV

Tailor your CV to the specific vacancy for which you are applying. While many people use a general CV designed to suit any position they are applying for, greater success can be achieved by tailoring your CV to the needs of the specific role for which you are applying. It stands to reason that every job and every organisation is different and every CV should, therefore, also be subtly different.

Supercharge Your CV

Want to land that next interview? Then, supercharging your CV could be the answer.

The purpose of a CV or résumé is to get you an interview. Yet half of all CVs need serious improvement. For most jobs, you've got just about six seconds of a recruiter's time to market yourself in a CV. Get it right and you'll improve your chances of landing an interview.

Make every second of reading time count in your favour. It's not difficult to have a better CV than most of your competitors.

Supercharging your CV involves taking these simple steps. Get them all right and your CV will put you in the best possible position to succeed.

Get A Professional Template

Professionally designed CV templates are more eye catching than text-heavy home-made ones. Good design and layout really can put your CV ahead of others. Microsoft Office has a good free CV template. You can also use your SEEK profile to develop an online résumé. If these don't appeal, then simply Google 'CV templates' and find one that suits you.

Use Bullet Points

Short, succinct bullet points are a good way of getting your message across. They're much easier to read than paragraphs of repetitive text. Bullet points allow recruiters to capture the essence of your experience at a glance.

Be Direct And Get To The Point

Simple, clear language is best in a CV; use active verbs instead of passive ones. Write: 'I managed a team of five people', instead of 'I was responsible for the management of a team of five'. Recruiters want to know your experience, former roles and responsibilities, skills, achievements and relevant education. They don't have time to read the detail of what you did in primary school or the details of your war gaming pastime.

Avoid Clichés

CVs are full of buzzwords, such as results-driven, team player, dynamic and many others. Show these attributes through your work experience.

Include Your Unique Selling Point (USP)

What makes you the right person for that job? If you don't have a spiel about why you're the right man or woman for the job, then spend some time working it out.

Explain The Gaps

Rather than paper over gaps in your employment, put a positive spin on them. This can help avoid any difficult questions at the interview stage. Make sure that your CV is consistent.

Get It Checked

Make sure you get your CV peer reviewed before firing it off to a recruiter. Ask friends, a professional or even a former school teacher of yours to check your CV for consistency, spelling and grammar. This matters to many employers.

Ask For Help

Good recruitment agencies will take the time to help you improve your CV.

Attend Workshops

Universities and institutes offer CV writing workshops and assistance. Take advantage of them. A few hours invested now could have long-term benefits for your career.

Tailor Your CV

Recruiters see a lot of CVs from overseas people that haven't been tailored for the market. What works in Beijing, London or New York, mightn't work here. For example, an IT candidate from the UK may be used to one or two page CVs, whereas here employers often want more detail and three pages would be more acceptable. Or a candidate may have been called a 'consultant' in their home country, but recruiters here are looking for someone with 'business analysis' experience when they are looking for a 'consultant'.

Presenting a good CV can truly make or break your chances of getting a job. The CV is your voice telling the prospective employer what makes you stand out from your competition. It also highlights your experience and qualifications. It is essentially a marketing tool that is selling you instead of a product.

In essence, your CV is the gateway to a job interview so it better be good.

Getting Organised

- **Organise the information:** Organise the information before getting started. Have all your dates and documents listed, prepared and handy for reference.

- **Plan the CV layout:** Set up a template or background for your CV. Design a heading at the top of the page and decide the format you will be using.

- **Examine the field:** Look at the field in which you are looking to get a job. Read some job ads for that field and use the information you find to determine what you need to include in your résumé.

- **Include relevant personal contact details:** Fill in your contact information. Name, address, email and phone number should all be neatly placed at the top of the page.

- **Verify the information:** Make sure that you verify all the information—dates, phone numbers and addresses.

- **Know the job requirements:** Know the requirements of the job for which you are applying. Make sure that when you list your responsibilities, you include tasks and skills that are relevant to the job applied for.

- **Decide on objectives:** Decide on what you want your professional, vocational research objective to be.

Academia and Achievements

- **Outline your academic qualifications:** Pick your stand-out qualifications and bullet point them under the relevant heading.

- **Include professional licenses:** List any professional licenses you have obtained that pertain to the job which you are applying.

- **List certifications:** Make a list of certifications that you have obtained that relate to the job you are applying for.

- **Give a synopsis of your education:** List your educational qualifications including your postgraduate, graduate and undergraduate degrees and studies.

- **Note relevant coursework:** Make note of relevant coursework that matches your objective. A study into modern financial practices would look great on a CV for a finance job.

- **Give your scientific research:** List any scientific research that you have done that relates to the job applied for. Even if you have non-relevant research, it is worth including as it is indicative of your overall suitability.

- **Detail academic research:** Academic research, laboratory experience and related skills from your days as a student should be included in this section of your CV.

- **Describe your thesis or dissertation:** Include a brief description of your thesis or dissertation. Include publications, papers or writings that have referenced your work.

- **Don't forget academic presentations:** List any academic presentations, along with any professional presentations that you have done. Your ability to give a presentation is especially important in corporate environment where speaking at meetings and conferences is a regular feature.

- **Talk about foreign language capabilities:** Include a list of foreign languages that you speak and your level of proficiency in them. This is gaining increasing importance in our global economy.

- **Be conclusive:** Add any information and qualifications you have that you feel pertain directly to your objective and support your CV.

Extra-curricular Activities

- **List your extra-curricular activities:** Include any extra-curricular activities that you feel are relevant. Activities, associations and memberships can be included. This is a further sign of your ability to interact in teams.

- **Mention community work:** Include a brief description of any community work that you have been part of, in the past or present, for instance, at your club house or with a youth association.

- **Mention your previous paid and voluntary work:** List your work experience, both paid and voluntary. Include what you did and what your responsibilities were.

- **Cultural awareness:** Mention your travel and cultural experiences.

Showing Your Skills

- **Skills make your CV memorable:** Know what skills make you stand out as a candidate. List those skills and highlight relevant qualifications.

- **Give details about your skills:** List your technical and specialised skills, including training related to these skills.

- **Be specific:** When you list your skills, don't be general; be specific. Anybody can say they are good at something, but saying that you are experienced or have an extensive knowledge conveys that you have done what you are saying and it is actually a skill, not just a CV filler.

- **Outline interests and ambitions:** Briefly describe your interests, include future academic and professional goals that you wish to accomplish.

- **Highlight skills gained through experience:** Highlight jobs and experience that make you stand out. Pick things that are relevant to what you are applying for and make them prominent.

- **Skills you offer:** When you are describing yourself, mention the things you brought to the table at previous jobs. List what makes you valuable to your current and your previous employers.

- **Utilise skill headers:** Use skill headings rather than job titles to list your experience. Often job titles can sound like they are unrelated to the job for which you are applying.

- **Focus on your strengths:** Highlight your strengths and minimise or leave out your weaknesses. Do this through formatting.
- **Tell the truth:** Don't embellish your assets, experience or qualifications. Be truthful and honest about all your accomplishments.

Writing And Formatting Your CV

- **Make a clear statement:** Make a statement about yourself. Decide ahead of time what you want your CV to say about you and put that into your CV.
- **Be descriptive:** Don't make blank statements. List the 'who', 'what', 'when' and 'where' of your experiences and information.
- **Remove the fluff:** Consider what is relevant information and what is not. Make a loose outline of what you feel needs to be included. Make a backup list for things that you will fit in, if you have space.
- **KISS—Keep it short, simple:** Keep your résumé simple, yet sharp, so that it catches your prospective employer's attention. Avoid busy fonts, logos and formatting, as they can be distracting and appear unprofessional.
- **Make it easy to read:** It is extremely important that your CV is easy to read. Make sure you choose a large enough font size so your reader isn't squinting. Have proper spacing; use bullets where acceptable.
- **Break up large blocks of text:** Add specific headings for things that will be of interest to your target audience. Things like languages, associations, skills, etc., are perfect items.

- **Stick to a consistent theme:** Keep a consistent theme throughout your CV. Don't include irrelevant information and experience.
- **Be concise and to the point:** Make sure your résumé is clear and understandable. Make sure you have a good idea of the message you are trying to convey, before you begin writing your CV.
- **Follow conventional writing rules:** Not everyone who writes a CV is a writer, but that is no excuse for sloppy work. Make sure that you follow all writing rules and that you are grammatically correct.
- **Sound interesting and proactive:** Use plenty of action verbs, so that you sound proactive. Using action verbs also helps in establishing that you will be making a contribution to your work place.
- **Check your punctuation and grammar:** Make sure that you use proper punctuation and number your pages, if required.
- **Use present tense when referring to current employment:** If you are still employed at your current job, make sure you use the present tense when describing your tasks and responsibilities.

Polish

- **Make your CV presentable:** Show that you want the job that you are applying for by making it known that you are interested. Make your CV as presentable as you can and let them know that they need you.

- **Place your name top and centre:** Make sure you use your name in the heading of your résumé and that it is listed at the top of all your CV pages.

- **Give your email address:** If you list your email on your CV, make sure that it is a professional email and not a silly email used for casual conversations. Open a new account using a free web-based service, if you have to.

- **Proofread to perfection:** Proofread your CV multiple times. Look for typos, incorrect grammar, inaccuracies, misplaced information and any improper or out-of-line formatting.

- **Third-party editing:** Have someone you trust read your CV. Ask them to check for typos, punctuation, formatting, clarity, relevance and ask them if it looks professional and relevant to what you are applying for.

- **Consider hiring a CV specialist:** Lastly, if you are having trouble coming up with a fresh, exciting and relevant CV, then consider hiring a specialist to help you. Alternatively, contact a friend or family member who has the experience of writing a CV.

- **Keep your CV under review:** We all know that life is one long chain of change, which should be reflected in your CV. Keep your CV up to date as you gain more experience, qualifications and licenses.

Writing a good CV takes time and dedication. It is essential that you prepare your CV properly and include all information relevant to the job for which you're applying. A CV differs from a résumé in that it is often more than one page. This is because of the fact that a CV is meant to highlight more of your academic information. You should still try to keep your CV as brief and relevant as possible, but it is acceptable for a CV to be longer than a résumé.

PERFECT APPRAISAL

Performance appraisal is the process of evaluating and documenting one's performance on the job. It is part of career development. *Perfect Appraisal* deals with:

- Appraisal process
- Training for appraisal
- Pitfalls in appraisals
- Dos and don'ts of appraisal

Perfect Appraisal provides simple techniques to a perfect appraisal with a holistic approach.

PERFECT ASSERTIVENESS

Assertiveness is important in all forms of communication. It is a way of relating to others that respects both your own and other people's needs, wants and rights. Aggressiveness provokes counter-aggression, assertiveness doesn't. *Perfect Assertiveness* spells out:

- Assertiveness training
- Responses: Passive, aggressive and assertive
- Effective communication
- Assertiveness skills
- Benefits of being assertive

Perfect Assertiveness helps you understand assertiveness as a life skill.

PERFECT COMMUNICATION

Communication is the process of sharing information, knowledge or meaning. What matters most is the 'response-ability'; response is more important than the message. Listeners must not just hear; they must listen. *Perfect Communication* deals with:

- Speaking skills
- Writing skills
- Listening skills

Perfect Communication is much more than just this.

PERFECT LEADER

If you want to inspire, motivate and engage, and move people into action, leadership is the ability you require. Leaders set direction and develop the skill to guide people to the right destination. *Perfect Leader* spells out:

- Leadership styles
- Initiatives that are needed
- Proactive tools
- The importance of perseverance
- Methods to step out of the comfort zone

Perfect Leader helps you to inspire the vision of the future as a leader. It equips you to make strategic decisions, shape conflict and find your competitive edge.

PERFECT MEETING

Meetings help one to build rapport. They are a forum for inter-learning and understanding; a platform to share information. *Perfect Meeting* is about the basic skills of management. It deals with:

- Effective meetings
- Conference meetings
- Stand-up meetings
- One-on-one meetings
- Tasks and skills of the chairperson

Perfect Meeting helps you generate cooperation and commitment to attain higher levels of performance.

PERFECT NEGOTIATION

In order to settle differences, one needs to master the skill of negotiation. Without this skill, conflicts and disagreements will arise. *Perfect Negotiation* deals with the process of negotiation and its different stages.

- Preparation
- Discussion
- Goals
- Win-win outcome
- Agreement

Perfect Negotiation helps you master the different types of negotiation formats, styles, and preparing strategies for negotiation.

PERFECT PRESENTATION

Presentation skills are critical as they help one to inform, motivate and inspire others. It is a means to get a message across to the listeners, with a persuasive element. *Perfect Presentation* talks about:

- Canons of persuasive presentations
- Verbal communication
- Non-verbal communication
- Styles of presentation
- Opening and closing of a presentation

Perfect Presentation helps you master the art of making effective presentations.

To Pea,

With

Aunty Theresa

lois

millie murray

Scripture Union, 207–209 Queensway, Bletchley, Milton Keynes,
MK2 2EB, England.
Email: info@scriptureunion.org.uk
Website: www.scriptureunion.org.uk

ISBN 1 85999 645 0

British Library Cataloguing-in-Publication Data. A catalogue record of this
book is available from the British Library.

Cover: Hurlock Design

Printed and bound in Great Britain by Bookmarque Ltd, Croydon, Surrey

I would like to thank Karen Haans, Librarian at St Martins-in-the-fields Girls School in Tulse Hill, for encouraging me to write this book.

My thanks also to Hilary Spurling and especially Steve Cook at the Royal Literacy Fund for their continuing support.

The name of the Lord is a strong tower
The righteous run to it and are safe.
Proverbs 18:10

Trust him at all times, O people;
Pour out your hearts to him,
For God is our refuge.
Psalm 62:8

1

'This is like living in hell!' I screamed. 'I hate it here!'

'It could be worse, Lois,' Mum said, holding on to her temper.

'Worse? Mum, you've got to be joking. What can be worse than this?' I shouted, loud enough for the whole neighbourhood to hear.

'Listen, love, we're all suffering from the change this move has caused, but we have to make the best of a bad situation, okay?' Mum's words had no effect. I stormed out of the kitchen, banging the door. The stairs took a battering as I flew up them two at a time. I slammed the bedroom door behind me, flung myself on my bed and cried with rage.

I tried to make sense of the last six weeks. My life had turned so upside down that my mind was still having trouble trying to put things in order. My thick, black hair hugged the back of my neck. I stroked it. Its rich silky texture usually calmed me. Not this time. I tried to overtake the bad feelings that were raging through me by breathing deeply. It didn't work.

I heard a light tapping at the door. I ignored it. 'Lois,' Dad called softly, 'can I come in?'

Hearing Dad's voice made me break out in a fresh bout of wailing. I bit my pillow to stem the awful noise that was escaping. Dad crept in, not waiting for me to invite him. He gently knelt his six foot three bulk down beside my bed. Stroking my hair softly, he said,

'Listen honey, this is only temporary. You know that I had no option but to take this shop and the upstairs flat. If I hadn't we would've been homeless. How would you have coped with that? Me and your mum with you and Niecy all living in one room in some nasty, smelly bed and breakfast place with ten other poor, homeless families, eh? I don't know about you, but I would have gone completely off my head. You would've all had to put me away in some nuthouse. At least living here will let me keep my head together.'

I tried to get a grip on myself so that I could listen to what Dad was saying. He continued, 'I'm hoping that at the most we will only have to be here for two years. After that I hope that we can move back to Hartenswood, or somewhere just as good.'

I sat up. The tears stopped for a moment, and my ears pricked up like a rabbit listening out for danger.

'What did you say, Dad? Two years? What do you mean, two years?'

I quickly swung my legs over the edge of the bed and stood up. Dad got up too, and tried to put his hands on my shoulders. I shoved him off, holding up my hands. 'Wait a minute, Dad.' I swallowed.

I tried to control my words, but they came out all wobbly as a wave of fear began to wrap itself around me. My left hand was on my hip, and my right was doing a bad job of trying to stem the tears that were gushing from my eyes. Sniffing, I asked Dad, 'Are you saying that we would have to spend two—' I held up two fingers, '—Two long, long years in this, in this…' Words failed me. I just couldn't find anything appropriate to say to fit how I was feeling. I knew I was being melodramatic, but I didn't care.

Dad took a step closer to me. I backed off, holding up my hand. He stopped. His jaw was twitching and I knew that he was trying to keep himself from exploding. He gulped, then said, 'Lois, as your father...' Dad never used the word 'father' unless he was well upset – he obviously was.

He pointed his finger at me and continued. 'As your father, this is the best that I can do for my family, okay? What happened before this time, and what happens after, is not in the equation. *Now,*' raised his voice, 'we all live here. And that's ¯' glared at me for a moment, then turned and l[ ] room. I knew then that I had used up all o[ ] patience and sympathy.

I crumpled to the floor, sobbing.

It seemed as though I had been crying for ages. My body felt stiff. I got up and looked in the mirror. My smooth, caramel complexion looked blotchy. My eyes were red and puffy. My lips, which are full and usually coated in lip-gloss, were cracked and dry. I tried to swallow, but my tongue felt as though it had doubled in size and was coated with sandpaper. My hair was in a state.

I was a mess.

Quickly brushing down my hair, I decided to go for a walk. I needed to get out, away from this dingy flat. At the bottom of the stairs I heard Mum calling me from the kitchen. I turned a deaf ear.

'I can't stop, Mum. See you later.'

'Lois, Lois, where do you think you're going?'

I rushed to the door, opened it and began clambering down the stairs. 'See you, Mum.'

'Lois!' shouted Mum. I ignored her.

My mind was numb, but my feet were moving fast as I walked along the road. I roughly knew where I was going. I haven't explored the area much, but I knew that not far from our flat was a green grassy area called Wayland Moss. If I kept walking through the thick grass it would take me near to my new school. I was to start Year 10 on Monday, the beginning of the autumn term.

A couple of black bags of rubbish blocked my path up ahead. I had to leap over them as they were strewn across the edge of the road. Broken glass was all over the pavement near the bags and crunched beneath my sandals as I delicately picked my way through. I shuddered as I narrowly missed stepping into dog's mess. I felt sick. I looked at the faces of some of the people that I passed, but their faces were blank. Was it me that was the odd one?

Walking the streets of Marshton Hills, I noticed that there were people of every nationality in the community. Walton Fields had a couple of different culture groups, but it was nowhere as diverse as Marshton Hills. Hartenswood had only one dominant culture group – and that was the money kind!

The long grass tickled my legs. Taking a short cut through Wayland Moss was a good idea. The wide space broke up the monotonous greyness of the streets. It seemed strange to have some greenery in the middle of an inner city area, but I suppose the town planners thought it would help keep the people sane! It was a nice sight amid the depressing squalor of the flats that boarded the grass verge.

Finally, after what seemed like ages, I came face to face with the school gates. The metal bars were covered in graffiti and secured with a very large chain and padlock. Was that to keep people out, or to lock the pupils in? The main school buildings and the smaller outer buildings appeared to be shrouded in a sort of greyness that was a stark contrast to the blue, late summer sky. Money was obviously short, as the whole outside of the school could do with some renovation to say the least.

This was to be my new school.

Sighing, I turned and walked along the road. Depression returned with a vengeance. I decided to walk back through the streets near the school. The immediate area was a mixture of flats and houses. I passed about three bus stops along the way, and at the fourth one I decided to sit down. I wanted to think about things and not be disturbed. At first I was the only one at the stop. The perspex glass was smashed, but I ignored it and sat down on one of the three orange plastic seats. A girl about my age came and stood in front of me. She was looking at the bus timetable. Even though she was wearing earphones, I could hear the tinny sound of the music. She turned and smiled at me and sat down.

Pulling out her earplugs and switching off her CD player, she said, 'Hi.'

I was a bit surprised. No one in the streets of Marshton Hills had acknowledged me since I moved here. Why start now? I shoved my hands deeper inside my jeans. I gave a quick smile and turned away from her.

'Have you been waiting long for the bus?' she asked.

I shook my head. I didn't want to talk.

'These 778s take forever, don't you think so?'

'I wouldn't know. I'm not from around here.' I spoke before I thought.

'Oh, really, where are you from?'

I didn't think that I would ever see this girl again, with her very long black and red braids, and her coffee cream skin that seemed to glow. So, taking a deep breath, I said, 'Hartenswood.'

'Hartenswood. I've heard of that place. Wow, your parents must be loaded.' She turned and looked at me.

'There aren't many black people living there?'

She looked at me, waiting for an answer.

'So?' I frowned. 'What's it to you?'

She sat up straight. 'Oh, I'm sorry if I offended you, I...'

'No, you didn't. Forget it.' I crossed my arms.

'What I meant was...'

'Forget it,' I said.

I heard her sigh deeply, then she said very quickly, 'Listen, I'm sorry that I've upset you, I really didn't mean anything bad by...'

Standing up, I turned and said, 'I'm not waiting for the bus, I was just sitting here minding my own business. That was until you came along and...'

The girl looked behind me. I glanced over my shoulder. Not seeing anything of interest, I continued to tell this girl just what I thought of her. I could hear a car roaring along the road towards us. I ignored it.

'...So you'll have to excuse me, as I have better things to do than to...'

All of a sudden, the girl jumped up and grabbed my arm. 'Quick, move!' she screamed.

I tried to free myself from her grip by pulling in the opposite direction. She was strong and determined. She hung onto me, dragging me into some bushes behind the bus stop.

'What is it?'

'Move, move, quickly!'

The panic in her voice and the fear in her eyes stopped me struggling. We tumbled down onto the ground. That instant I heard a loud crash. The ground shook with the impact. I thought it was an earthquake. The noise stopped my mouth in mid-sentence. Fear caused me to clutch hold of the girl's hand. The perpetual beeping of a car alarm pierced the air.

The girl stood up. Shakily, I stood up too, in time to see three boys get out of the car. They opened the door of the driver's side, and dragged an Asian boy out.

'My leg, my leg!' squealed the boy.

'Don't worry about your leg, we've got to get away from here,' said the tall black boy. The other two boys, one black and the other white, began to run up the road, calling 'C'mon, c'mon!'

The tall black boy hooked his arm under the young Asian boy's arm and helped him along the road. Time stood still. The boys were making their getaway as the girl and I watched them. I was too stunned to do anything. The girl pulled out her mobile phone and began to punch in numbers. 'Hello, police please.' She led me a little way away from the scene of the crash.

I was too overwhelmed by what I had just witnessed to resist.

Was this a taste of what my life would now be like?

2

'Mum, I don't need you to drive me to school. I'd rather catch a bus or walk than have you take me.'

'Lois, this is your first day, and I'm taking you whether you like it or not. So just get yourself ready, and hurry up.'

The clouds were emptying themselves with a vengeance. The sky was grey. The sun was nowhere to be seen. What a day to start school! The weather was having no effect on Mum. She was determined that we left for school right away.

The tone of her voice let me know that her mind was made up. Reluctantly, I finished getting dressed. I had been dreading this morning, and had tried to think of different ways that I could put off the inevitable. Pretending to be ill was the only thing that I thought might work. But Mum, who used to be a nurse, couldn't be fooled easily. I knew it would be far easier to just get on with it.

It wasn't hard for me to work out why Mum was being so protective. When I had got home after witnessing that awful accident, I was in such a state. My hair was wild, my face was crusty with dried tears, and I was hysterical.

Babbling incoherently, Mum was barely able to understand me.

'I…I…I…was…bus stop, a car… an accident,' I sobbed into her arms.

'What was you doing at the bus stop?' Mum screamed. She didn't wait for me to reply. She steamrollered on, 'An accident, oh my goodness!' Mum clutched me tightly. She ran her hands up and down my back, checking to feel if I had broken any bones. Then she held me at arms' length by my shoulders. 'Are you alright, are you hurt anywhere, shall I call a doctor?'

I tried to tell her I was fine, but she got a bit carried away and wasn't listening. I think it was more to do with the fact that I looked such a state!

It was such a dreadful experience.

That evening Mum, Dad and I went over the whole scenario again and again. The police had questioned Tia and I at the scene of the crime. They had also wanted us to go to the police station to look through some photos to perhaps see if we could identify the culprits.

I told them straight away that because events had happened so quickly, I doubted whether I would be able to recognise any of their faces from a hole in a paper bag! That didn't go down very well. Tia said her memory was a bit hazy too. The truth for me was that I could clearly recall the face of the tall black boy, and the Asian boy. But there was absolutely no way that I was going to pick out their photographs if they were on file. I reasoned that just as I remembered them, they'd probably remember me. My mind jumped at the thought of giving evidence in court against them. Then they'd probably end up having some sort of vendetta against me.

Forget it!

* * *

Mum had driven the car round to the front of the

shop. I didn't want to get in, but what else could I do? The 'car' was a clapped out silver-grey Volvo estate. I think it must have been one of the first models off the production line, it was so ancient. Dad said it was perfect for ferrying his stock from the wholesalers to the shop. Mum never said a word. When I think of what we used to drive, I find it hard to believe that Mum and Dad have accepted this old banger and our new way of life so quickly!

Mum eased the car into the flow of the traffic as I fought back tears that were threatening to gush out.

'So, how you feeling, nervous?' asked Mum.

Shrugging my shoulders I looked out the window. A tear had escaped and was cruising down my cheek. Brushing it away, I sniffed and began to dig around in my bag to detract Mum's attention. Mum stroked my arm. Softly she said, 'I feel for you darling, I really do, but there's nothing that I can do to change this school situation, or our way of life now.'

I nodded. I knew what Mum had said was true. If she were able to afford the fees to keep me at the Academy she would have done, and I would have gladly travelled the distance every day.

But she couldn't afford it and neither could Dad, so here I was.

It seemed as though we were only in the car for a few minutes before the wire fence that enclosed the school loomed into view. Streams of young people filtered through the gates. Most of them were wearing the school colours of navy blue trousers or skirts, with white blouses or shirts. The blazer was navy blue with the school badge on the pocket. Others wore a multitude of colours. Mum managed to squeeze the car into a space outside the school. It was tight. Turning the engine off, she said, 'Listen, Lois, there's no reason why you shouldn't do well at this school. University is still on, and hopefully by then our lives will be different. We might have moved into a better area by then.'

A watery smile ghosted my lips. I knew Mum was trying to cheer me up, and I really, really wished I could be optimistic like her. But the truth of the matter was, on this particular morning, I felt like I was entering an arena of lions and I didn't know whether they were going to be friendly or not.

I didn't have to wait long to find out.

The Head's secretary told us to sit outside the Head's office. We were there for what seemed like ages. Every so often Mum turned and smiled at me. I suppose that was to reassure me, but it didn't stop my stomach knotting up. My mind drifted off. I wondered what was happening at my old school. First thing on a Monday morning was English Lit. There had been eighteen girls in my class, including me. Mrs Benton was a really good teacher and I had enjoyed her classes. I had promised Sophie that I would email her later that evening and tell her all about my first day. Well, I'd probably tell her that the first half of the day was spent outside the Head's office.

'Lois! What are you doing here?' asked an incredulous voice.

Focusing my eyes on a slightly familiar face, I was horrified when the realisation of who it was kicked in.

'Tia!' I said, mortified.

'You know each other!' said Mum, with obvious delight in her voice. 'This is really wonderful, Lois.

You didn't tell me that you knew someone at your school. Now this will put my mind at rest. How do you know each other?'

Tia and I looked at each other. Tia was waiting for me to answer, but my tongue was temporarily paralysed and I couldn't speak. It turned out I didn't have to.

'Mrs Darnell? Lois?'

We all turned in the direction of the voice. It was the Head's secretary. Smiling, she said, 'This way, please. The Head will see you now.'

We followed her into the Head's office. Mum said goodbye to Tia. I ignored her.

'Welcome to Marshton Hills Community School!' beamed Mrs Wilson, the Headmistress.

Mrs Wilson was totally hyperactive. She had shocking dyed red hair, with matching lips. I was mesmerised by her mouth, even though I wasn't paying any attention to what she was saying.

The meeting was over in what seemed like a few minutes. We were up and out of her office and marching quickly through the corridors of the school. I tried not to look at my surroundings but it was hard not to. The place was a mess. Pictures that had been put on the walls to show the pupils' workmanship were torn or written on. Furniture that was in need of repair was dotted about the corridors. Students who seemed to be lost were hanging around too. Without directly looking at them, Mrs Wilson issued orders at every person we passed.

'Bradley, you're supposed to be in Science for this period. Meet me outside my office in ten minutes.'

'Deepinder, your parents haven't contacted me yet,

why? I'll call them again today.'

She whizzed passed them, not stopping to catch her breath, with Mum and I hot on her heels.

Finally, we stopped outside a door. Mrs Wilson turned to me and said, 'Lois, this is 10AR. Your teacher is Ms Levine, who is also head of Year 10. In you go.'

I couldn't move. Through the door window I could see that every eye was on me. Ms Levine had stopped talking and was looking at me too through her thick-lens spiral glasses. She looked like a tiny bird that was perching on the edge of the world – just about to fall off.

Tentatively, I opened the door. I didn't dare look at Mum as I felt I would turn tail and run as far away from this place as I possibly could.

'Bye, Lois.' Mum's voice was hardly audible as I stepped into the hot classroom. The door closed behind me, and I knew then that I was on my own.

'Hello,' smiled Ms Levine. 'You must be Lois Darnell. This is class 10AR. Please find a seat over the back there.' She pointed vaguely. I did my best to follow her lead. I sat down next to a pretty Asian girl, whose shoulder-length shiny black hair gleamed with health. I smiled at her. She snatched her bag from the chair as I was just about to sit down. The look she gave me was poisonous. I glanced at the person to the left of me. A tall black girl looked me up and down, and then turned her back on me. She came across as mysterious and dangerous. My stomach flipped over a few times, and goosebumps pricked my skin. Looking straight ahead at Ms Levine wasn't easy for me, either. The young black guy in front of me turned around and was staring at me with his tongue hanging out of his mouth. Then he began to lick his lips, staring at me all the while. He made me think of the wolf in the Little Red Riding Hood story. I was trying hard to hold myself together. But the hostility that permeated the air was beginning to suffocate me, and it seemed more concentrated where I was sitting. The noise level in the classroom had steadily got louder. Ms Levine had to shout so that she could be heard.

The boy in front leaned closer to me and said, 'Lois. Nice name. You look like you need some sorting out.' He winked. 'Know what I mean? I'll meet you after school and eh, and eh, we can give things a go, alright?' He looked me over and said 'Nice, nice.' He winked again.

The girl next to me laughed. The girl on my left grabbed my arm. 'Listen.' She pointed to the laughing boy in front. 'Tufar is my best friend's man right, and when I tell her that you have been messing with him, your life won't be worth living,' she spat out between clenched teeth.

I wanted to tell her that she'd got it wrong, that it was him not me, but my mouth was fixed, my jaw was locked, and words that were usually quick out of my mouth were frozen somewhere in my chest cavity.

A buzzer sounded and chairs were scraped across the floor in the haste to get out of the classroom.

Tufar was up and out the door just as quick, without giving me a backward glance. The black girl and the Asian girl and myself were the only ones left.

Ms Levine walked over to us wearing a large smile. 'Oh, Jennifer and Neera, isn't that kind of you to look after Lois on her first day. Why don't you take her to the tuck shop for a quick snack? After break-time you can take her to your next lesson.'

Jennifer smiled at Ms Levine and said it would be no problem. I didn't have time to protest against this plan as both Jennifer and Neera held each of my arms and escorted me out the door.

At the threshold, Ms Levine quickly added, 'Lois, Marshton Hills is a far cry from Hartenswood, but I'm sure you'll really like it here.' She smiled.

I shuddered as both my escorts held onto my arms even tighter and walked me out of the door and along the corridor.

3

'How much money do you have?' asked Neera.

I wasn't sure if she was talking to Jennifer or me, so I didn't answer her. I soon found out.

'Are you deaf or something?' Neera tugged my arm.

My mind raced as I realised that, depending on my answer, this situation could get totally out of control. I knew that I was in a dangerous position.

'Why?' I quavered.

'No, I don't want you to ask me why, I just want to know how much your rich parents gave you to spend this morning. Do you understand me now?' barked Neera.

'I don't know how much,' I whispered.

'Well. We'll have to find out then, won't we?' Jennifer looked at me, still holding onto my arm.

We had left the main building now, and were walking across the yard. Raindrops were spitting down on us. Ahead were some portacabins that were used as extra classrooms. I really hoped that we were not going to be the only ones there. There were pupils milling around us, and I desperately wanted to cry out for help. But I couldn't. When they spotted Jennifer and Neera, they quickly scooted off. That only added to my fear. I had tried to resist them by pulling back and by trying to shake off their hands, but Jennifer in particular was one tough cookie. I felt as though she had some personal malevolent feelings towards me.

But why?

We stopped at the last portacabin that was as far away from the main school building as possible. This is it, I thought, they're going to do their worst to me here. I resigned myself to the thought that at least if they got whatever they were going to do to me over with as quickly as possible, then perhaps I could just go back to my class.

Or was that wishful thinking?

Entering the portacabin, the smoky atmosphere caught me by surprise. I had hoped that we wouldn't be alone, but I certainly wasn't expecting their friends.

'Why've you brought her here, Jennifer, eh?' A white girl was speaking. Her complexion was like cream, she had wonderfully prominent high cheekbones, and her blonde cane row plaits were neatly tied, hanging down her back. She inhaled deeply on her cigarette and asked Jennifer again, 'Well. Why, Jennifer?'

'Cos she was chatting up *your* Tufar, that's why.' Jennifer laughed and the other girls that were there joined in.

The girl got off the table – she wasn't smiling. She walked towards me and stood right in front of me, and I wanted to faint. The whole room was charged with such a volatile atmosphere that it seemed combustible.

She inhaled from her cigarette. 'So, you like my man, do you?'

I couldn't speak. Without moving, my eyes quickly glanced at the group of girls and I saw Jennifer and Neera talking to another black girl, who was staring at me.

'Well?' said the high cheek-boned girl, 'is it true that you were eyesing up my guy?' She pointed her finger in my face.

'Ellie, ask her how much money she's got,' shouted the girl that Jennifer and Neera had been talking with.

Ellie dropped her cigarette on the floor and ground it out with her shoe. 'Right then. How much?' she held out her hand.

The other girls slowly began to walk towards me. I took a step back, and one of the girls quickly went and stood by the door. I was like a mouse trapped by a pack of ferocious cats.

'Please, look, I haven't got much,' I said, trembling as the vice of fear gripped me tighter. I held out my bag, tears spilled down my cheeks, and my bladder was threatening to empty its contents. Normally, when faced with danger, I would boldly confront it. But this was something completely out of my league. My head was swimming.

Suddenly, the door swung open and I heard a voice shout, 'What's going on in here?'

The black girl said, 'Get out, Tia, it's nothing to do with you, right.'

'Oh yes it has, Carmel.'

I turned round quickly and just the sight of Tia gave me a little bit of hope and self-respect.

Carmel stepped towards Tia, who seemed not in the least bit afraid of her, and said, 'Listen, if you think your *Jesus* and you churchy carryings-on is going help you, you thought wrong.' Their faces were inches apart.

Tia side-stepped Carmel and said to me, 'C'mon Lois, let's go.'

I didn't have to be asked twice. I moved quicker than an electrical current. I was out the door, breathing in fresh air.

Carmel and her friends didn't make any effort to stop me. I was puzzled yet glad at the same time.

Carmel stuck her head out of the door. 'Lois, your guardian angel won't always be around.' She stared long and hard at Tia and I.

I made to run – I wanted to get as far away as possible, but Tia said, 'Don't run. Walk. Let's take our time. We don't want to give them the impression you're scared.'

I was just about to look back when Tia grabbed my arm. 'No, you mustn't. Don't pay them any attention.'

My stomach started to contract. Just as we turned the corner, I puked. Tia jumped back in the nick of time otherwise she would have been covered. I held on to the wall, and retched up the contents of my stomach. Slowly, I stood up and took a few deep breaths, wiping my mouth with a tissue that Tia had handed me.

'How are you feeling?' enquired Tia.

Weakly smiling, I said, 'Not too bad. Much better than I felt in there.' I nodded my head in the direction of the portacabin. We resumed our walk towards the main building and safety.

Usually I hate getting wet in the rain, but this time it was different. The sense of freedom as the raindrops fell on my head and ran down my face was exhilarating. Added to my puking, it was quite cathartic.

By the time we had got to the main building, I was trying to feel my normal self. I paused to catch my breath. Then I burst into tears. Hugging me, Tia said, 'It's okay, Lois, it's okay.'

I cried even more. Deep down I somehow knew that it wasn't going to be okay. I knew that I had made enemies of Carmel and her friends, and I didn't know how. I also had no idea what to do about it.

'Tia, I don't think I'm going to be able to go to any classes today. But,' I paused, 'but, I don't want to go home, either.'

Tia smiled. It made her look quite pretty. 'I understand. Look, I'll take you to see Mrs Crofton. She's sort of the school nurse-cum-counsellor-cum-shoulder-to-cry-on-person. I seen her a few times myself.'

Alarmed, I cried, 'I don't want anyone to know about what happened. You won't tell anyone, will you?' I pleaded.

Placing her arm around my shoulder, Tia said, 'Of course, I won't tell a soul, if that's what you want.'

'It is.' My heart was thudding. I couldn't bear the thought of people knowing that I had been bullied by a group of girls. It was more than embarrassing.

'I just thought that you could tell her that you weren't feeling too good, but you didn't want to go home just yet.'

'Oh, that's fine.' I smiled weakly.

'I hope you don't think I'm interfering, but would you like to come and sit in the sixth form common room, and I'll make you some coffee? I've got a free period.'

'Yes, please,' I said with such relief that it flew out of my mouth like a rush of wind.

'That settles it then.'

Briskly, Tia marched off. I was close behind her. She stopped at an office door and knocked.

'Come in,' said a voice.

Tia pushed me in front of her and stepped into the office behind me. 'Mrs Crofton, this is Lois Darnell and she started school today, but she's feeling unwell. Is it possible for her to spend a bit of time in the sixth form room?'

Mrs Crofton smiled at me. She looked as though she was near retirement age and she had an air of calmness and tranquility about her. Looking over her half-moon glasses at me, she said in a gentle voice, 'Hello dear, come in and sit down.' I slid into the chair facing her desk. She looked up at Tia who said, 'I'll just wait outside.'

Mrs Crofton nodded at her and smiled again at me. 'So, what's the problem?'

My mind was racing, searching out words that wouldn't get me onto the subject of bullying. 'I, eh, eh, felt nauseous, eh, and I vomited.'

'Hmm,' she said. 'Have you a boyfriend, Lois?'

I immediately knew what she meant – could I be pregnant?

'No, I haven't.'

'Good.'

She asked me a few questions about my old school. Then she said, 'Ms Levine is your head of year, dear?'

'Yes, she is.'

'Right then, I'll let her know that you won't be attending classes for the rest of the day. Are you sure you don't want to go home. I can phone your parents, will someone be there for you?'

'No,' I said a bit too quickly, but the last thing I wanted was for Mum or Dad to know that I was feeling bad. Mum, who would make a good interrogation officer, would probably wheedle it out of me, and everything would be blown out of proportion.

Mrs Crofton sat there looking at me for a moment, before she said, 'Is there anything else that you would like to tell me?'

'No.'

'Okay, Lois.' She paused then said, 'This school is probably worlds away from your previous one. These pupils have different needs and expectations. You have to be strong to survive here, believe me.' Her smile brightened up her face and she said that I could go. As I got to the door she said, 'Lois, if you do have any problems, just come and see me.'

I nodded and slipped out the door quickly. Tears were pricking my eyes, and I didn't want Mrs Crofton to see them.

Tia took one look at the fear and anguish on my face and grabbed my arm. 'C'mon, let's walk.'

4

'... It was my transformation that finally convinced my mum that what I was now into was something that was for good.'

Tia was telling me about how she first became a Christian. I had heard nothing like it in my life.

The rain had stopped, leaving a shiny, glistening covering, like baby oil, across the tarmac yard. I had drunk two cups of strong coffee, and sitting in the comfortable, warm sixth form common room made my recent troubles seem far away. There was only one student using the room. A tall black guy wearing headphones was poring over his folder at one of the tables and shaking his head in time to the beat. I was glad that there weren't a lot of other people around – most people were probably at their classes. That meant that Tia and I could talk freely.

'So, what do you think, Lois?'

'I, eh, nice,' I nodded. Tia looked at me, and she knew that I hadn't really been listening. Lowering my eyes, I mumbled, 'I'm sorry, I was miles away.'

'I'm sorry too, I get so passionate about my faith that I become so carried away that I forget the person I'm talking to.'

'My mum's a Christian.'

Tia's eyes lit up like sparklers. 'Really? That's great. Have you never thought of becoming one yourself?'

'But I am one.' I had to admit that even though I had gone to Sunday school as a child, since I had reached my teens, the appeal of church was very low on the list of my priorities.

'Really?' Tia said unbelievingly. 'So, when did you get baptised then?'

'I haven't. I mean, when I say that I'm a Christian, it means that I believe in God. That's all you need, isn't it? You don't have to go to church or anything like that, just believe. Anyway, I'm not interested in going to church or anything like that. Right now I've got other problems that I need to sort out.'

Tia had been standing by the window, but she made her way towards me and sat in the chair next to me.

'This situation with Carmel and co can be resolved you know.' Tia looked at me knowingly.

'How?' At last, Tia seemed to be talking sense. She had finally got my full attention.

'Well, you said your mum was a Christian, she only has to pray to Jesus and through his power, he will right the wrong.'

I looked at Tia for a long moment. 'You're mad. How could anyone in the twenty-first century believe in such nonsense, especially with all this street violence and war and modern technology, not to mention girls who want to kick your head in?'

Seeming oblivious to what I had said, Tia rattled on. 'Over and over again the Bible talks about how God comes to the rescue of his people and how they are able to overcome their problems. I mean, look at me, when Carmel and I were so close, people thought we were sisters, and…'

My ears pricked up. 'You and Carmel were close?

You mean *that* Carmel?' I pointed my thumb towards the door. 'Carmel who's just scared the life out of me,' I continued, 'whose middle names must be Rambo and Hannibal? *That* Carmel?' I shouted, half out of my chair.

Nodding her head Tia repeated, 'Yes, yes, that Carmel. Anyway—'

I held up my hand, and shook my head as if to clear the confusion that Tia's words had caused. I asked her to explain.

She did.

'Carmel and I go right back to Nursery. We lived in each other's houses. I suppose you could say that we were like sisters. In fact, people said that we even looked alike, although I am two years older than her, and her complexion is different to mine.' Tia stopped talking and looked down at her fingernails. I knew she was thinking about something, maybe a painful memory, which wouldn't surprise me with a friend like Carmel. But then again, it could be thoughts of happier times.

'Okay, so?' I was eager for her to carry on.

Sighing and still looking at her hands, Tia said, 'We saw each other every single day for years and years. Her dad left her mum who had to bring up Carmel and her brother alone. Her dad was a very violent man. He had been in prison for violent crimes too. My mum and dad were still together for a few years after that.'

She stopped again.

Anger was mounting up inside me and I wanted to grab Tia and drag the rest of the story out of her. I clenched and unclenched my fists. Gritting my teeth,

I said crossly, 'Well, are you going to tell me?'

Jerking her head up, Tia gazed at me. For a moment I thought she was going to cry, but she quickly swallowed and her words rushed out of her mouth like a runaway train. 'My dad just upped and left us. One day he was there and the next he was gone. It was worse than him actually dying.' She got up quickly and offered me another cup of coffee.

'Oh, I'm sorry, Tia.' My hand flew up to my mouth and guilt punctured my irritation.

Tia turned to face me. 'I was eleven and Carmel was ten. Our mums had been close too, up until that point. It was a few months later when Mum discovered that Dad had been telling some of his plans to Carmel's mum, and to make matters worse, they had had a short affair. It really cut my mum up. The betrayal. The lies. And all the time my mum was telling Carmel's mum all her business. You can imagine the shock of my mum finding this out. Mum had to drag the information out of Carmel's mum, and by that time, when she tried to contact my dad, he had gone. Obviously, Mum sussed that her and Carmel's mum, Linda, were not such good friends after all. Within a year we had moved. Carmel and I were still friends all that time, until eighteen months ago.'

'Why, what happened?'

'I became a Christian, wasn't you listening to me?'

What could I say? I shook my head. 'Sorry, I had a lot on my mind.'

Tia smiled. 'Don't worry, I understand. You see, for the first few years of coming to this school, I was full of anger and bitterness about my dad leaving us. I didn't go to lessons and I was totally disruptive. I was

B-A-D. Carmel and I was Sisters-in-Crime. My mum was threatened by the authorities with court action if I didn't go to school. Mum tried all kinds of tactics. She started to come to school with me, she would phone me on my mobile a hundred times a day. Mum even had me followed by her friends. I still bunked off nearly every day! Mum would somehow know, and wherever I was, Mum or one of her friends would spring out from behind a corner. I would be dragged kicking and screaming to school. It was a nightmare.'

'Then what happened?' Tia really had my full attention now.

'It was weird really. My friends and I were in a café having a cup of tea and some toast one afternoon when we should've been at school. A young couple came in and sat near us. Carmel and I and a few others were puffing on our cigarettes and having a laugh, when the girl turned and said to me, 'You're Tia Affley.' I wondered how she knew me. She explained that she was an old neighbour, and she also recognised Carmel. She was a total stranger to me, but she was able to recall certain things about us when we were younger and I sort of remembered her then. She looked so different. Debbie, that's her name, told us she was a Christian and invited us to church.'

'So you went to church and the rest is history.'

Tia nodded. 'Sort of. Anyway. I feel and know that I am a different person now. I feel at peace with myself.'

'What about Carmel, though?'

'I'm still praying for her.'

Folding my arms I retorted, 'Your prayers are obviously not working.'

'Some things take time.'

'Which is something I haven't got. I need action now.' I bashed the armchair with my fist.

Tia sat next to me and placed her hand on my arm. 'Things will change for the better and...'

I jumped out of my chair. 'What are you now, a predictor of the future? Shall I call you "Madame Tia" or something?' I shouted. I just couldn't control my temper. My emotions rollercoasted from moment to moment.

Tia stood up. 'Listen, Lois. Carmel and any other problems you may have won't go away by being fired up and angry all the time. Crying and self-pity won't help either.'

I sat down. With my head in my hands I whispered, 'What am I going to do? I'm so frightened.' The gentle pitter-patter of the raindrops on the window was the only sound that could be heard for a short while. A few more students came in, laughing and talking. I sat up.

'Hi Tia,' they chorused.

She smiled and gave a slight wave. 'What's so funny?' she asked. A girl with a near-shaven head began to tell Tia about some incident. I switched off. The common room was a safe haven for me. The thought of leaving the safety of the room filled me with dread. What if I met up with Carmel between here and home? The only possible way out of this situation was to run away. It seemed the best option at the moment.

The noise level rose as the group of students made themselves drinks and sat around the room.

'You know something, Lois?' said Tia, giving me

her full attention. 'When I was running with the pack, whenever we picked on someone, if they gave in to fear we would make their lives a misery. But if the victim stood up for themselves, we'd back off.' Tia looked at me and saw my disbelief.

'It's true. You know Neera? That's how she joined the gang. Carmel and the girls gave her hell, but she stood up to it and now look, she's one of them.

'The other thing about Carmel and people like her is that you must never, ever show that you're scared. That's like a drug to them. They feast off it and get strong on it. And then that's just the beginning of your sorrows. Believe me, I know.'

* * *

'Where's Mum?'

'She's gone to a job interview. Lois, I want you to mind and shut the shop for me. I have to go to the bank.'

'Job interview? Mum's getting a job? Doing what?'

'Nursing,' replied Dad.

'But she hated it when she used to do it.'

'We need the money. Look, Lois, you know how to use the till, don't you? I shan't be long.'

'But Dad, I—'

'Lois, you'll be fine. I've got to go. You can tell me all about school later. See you, love.' Dad rushed out of the door and was gone.

My mind was spinning like a roller blade. Since we had moved to this shop, I'd only worked in it once or twice, and that was under duress! Mum and Dad usually did it between them. I hated it. When we lived in Hartenswood, Dad had employed two or three people in each of his shops. I'd never been needed.

Marshton Hills was different.

I sat at the counter and thought about my life, my family and how everything had changed since we moved.

My elder sister Eunice, or Niecy as she prefers to be called, was studying at Kings College University in London. She reckons that she hated Hartenswood. 'It's so pretentious,' was her favourite phase. I remember how, one supper time, she made a big deal about the Art teacher at the Academy.

'He told me I was an exotic creature, in front of the whole class, as though I was some jungle animal. I told him that I'm a young black woman, and proud of the fact.' She was working herself up into such a state that Mum had to calm her down. Niecy is easily excited.

Mum's face popped into my mind. I wondered how she was feeling about having to go back to a job she hated. I'm surprised that she's seriously thinking of working again. But lately, Mum seems to have changed a bit. Her face doesn't look so pinched and worried. In fact, she seems a lot more calm and together. I'd even go as far as to say she seems happier. Does she *like* living in Marshton Hills?

I shook my head. How could she? It was hell on earth compared to where we used to live.

My mind shifted onto Sophie, my best friend. I wondered what she was up to.

Ten minutes later, I was totally bored. Not one customer had entered the shop to distract me. I was tempted to go upstairs and make myself something to eat and drink, but I thought that if I did, a dozen customers would come in and probably help themselves to Dad's stock.

I decided to phone Sophie instead, and find out what was happening down in Hartenswood. She answered on the first ring – she had her own line.

'Hi, Sophie.'

'Hi, Lois!'

Hearing Sophie say my name lifted me, and I injected some false gaiety into my voice.

I told her about the joyriders and the police. 'Oh, Lois, that's amazing!' Sophie exclaimed. 'You're really in the thick of things down there, nothing exciting ever happens up here, you know that. Wait until I tell the others, they'll be green with envy.'

Even though I love Sophie dearly – she's my closest friend – she can be so vacuous at times.

'Please, please, please invite us down to see you, Lois. What about next weekend? I'll cancel shopping with Mummy.'

'No, not next week, Sophie, I've got a lot on.' To divert her from the subject of visiting me I told her in not too fine a detail about Carmel and co. She commiserated with me then said, 'You have to stand up to them, Lois. Remember when Holly Bracknell and her horrid friends started to pick on you and call you names? You really dealt with her, leaving her in a floods of tears. She kept away from you after that. Anyway, how's the local talent?'

'Sophie, I hardly know anyone.'

'Simon Pascal is sooo divine, Lois,' she rattled on. 'He called here for Edward on Saturday, and he kept on looking at me with his huge, blue speckled eyes. You know, I think his eyes are his best feature. I could just simply fall into them and float away.' Sophie sighed.

A woman with a little boy came into the shop.

'Sophie, I have to dash now, but I'll call you later in the week, bye.' I replaced the handset and attended to the customer. The woman was very, very fussy. She wanted a pair of trainers for the little boy and she had me show her nearly all the pairs that we had in stock that were the little boy's size. Then she told me that she didn't like any of them and upped and left. I was angry. Because I didn't put each pair of trainers back after I had shown the customer, I now had the task of matching the odd trainer with its partner in the box. Why had this woman bothered to come into the shop in the first place?

I was getting more annoyed by the minute and I wished I had given the woman a piece of my mind. Whilst I was in the back of the shop putting away the last few boxes, I heard the door go.

'I won't be a minute,' I called.

Hurriedly, I put the boxes on the shelf. My mood was foul and I wasn't in a good frame of mind to be pleasant to anyone.

I called out before I went back into the shop. 'Yes, what do you want?'

On seeing whom my 'customers' were, my mouth flew open in shock, but I quickly recovered and shut it.

It was Carmel and Ellie. They were shocked too. I was sure that they could hear my heart thumping in my throat, but in a split second I decided that I had to be strong like Tia and Sophie had said.

This was make or break time for me.

I had to make sure that I was going to come through this.

5

For a nanosecond we stood looking at each other. I spoke first. 'What do you want?'

I detected a flicker of surprise in Ellie, so with my heart thumping in my throat and my hand on my hip (to steady myself) I pushed ahead with, 'Have you come into this shop to buy something or not?' I hoped that my false bravado wasn't apparent to them.

'Yeah we have, *actually*,' piped up Ellie. 'I want to see those trainers in size four please.' She pointed to a pair of Nikes. The price tag was £89.99. I felt sure that she didn't have the money, and before the words were formed in my mind, they flew out of my mouth. 'Have you got the money?' I turned towards the stockroom not waiting for her answer. I didn't want them to see that fear had quickly taken over my sassiness. 'Size four is it?'

In the stockroom I groped the shelf. My stomach contracted for the second time that day, but I had to force the coffee mixed with bile down. This was not the time to be sick. Quickly swallowing deep breaths, I found the trainers. As soon as I entered the shop, I intuitively knew that things had changed – for the worse. Carmel walked over to me and snatched the box out of my hand. I should have said something, but momentarily I couldn't. I could feel my bravery slipping through my fingers and oozing down to the floor. Clenching my hands to regain some strength,

I said, 'Are you going to sit down and try them on?'

'Yeah, when I'm ready, alright?' After a few seconds, Ellie sat and took off her old trainer and tried the new one on.

Carmel put her hands on her hips. 'So, nice little job you've got here. How much do they pay you?'

That riled me a bit and I retorted, 'None of your business.'

They both looked at each other and laughed. 'Ohhh,' smiled Ellie, 'who's got it together now?'

Carmel sauntered over to me. Our noses were nearly touching. Slowly she mouthed, 'I asked you how much?'

Holly Bracknell's face flashed in front of Carmel's and I shouted, 'Listen, right, if you don't want to buy anything, get out!' Holding back my tears was tough. I rushed to the door and held it open, swallowing to keep the fear and panic from jumping out.

'Did you hear?' I shouted, more to keep myself strong than to frighten them. I was surprised to see Ellie putting her trainer back on.

Carmel piped up. 'You know, it would be handy to have a friend who worked in a shop like this. What do you reckon, Ell? A good discount for our trainers or even a free pair now and again.'

'Sounds like just what the doctor ordered,' smiled Ellie. My stomach lurched. But before another word was spoken by Carmel, Ellie or myself, my dad stormed through the open door. 'Would you believe it?' he shouted. He crashed his briefcase down on the counter before opening it and pulling out some plastic moneybags. Dumping the money into the cash register he said, 'That bank manager, he wants to see me fail. He's taking every single penny that I'm earn-ing. Interest rates, bank charges. What do I care about rates? This is my *business*, my *livelihood*!' He thumped the counter so loudly I thought it would snap in two. Carmel and Ellie weren't hanging around to listen to the ravings of an irate shop owner. They rushed through the door without a word to me. I was glad.

Dad's mood grew darker by the second. I told him that I would make him some coffee, and sought refuge in our kitchen.

Dad accepted his cup gratefully, but I didn't stay around to hear any more about his escapades at the bank.

Lying in bed with my duvet cover pulled up close around my neck, I felt warm and safe. I had Roly, my teddy bear which I had had since I was about two years old, in bed with me. I had discarded him when I was eleven, and from that point on he had lived in our loft. Until, that is, I was sorting through different things in the loft, as we were preparing to move, and had found him again. Since then, he has shared my bed and my thoughts, heartache and secrets.

'Roly, what am I going to do?' I whispered in his ear. His smiling face comforted me, but I wished, for this time at least, that he could talk and advise me on what course of action I should take. I was in two minds whether or not to tell Mum about Carmel and co. She would want not only to take me to school, but she'd sit with me in all my classes! But how long could she do that? And what would happen to me after she left?

Of all the things I'd imagined about my new school, being bullied wasn't one of them. I knew that maybe some of the girls wouldn't like me. I thought that I might be lucky and meet a girl who would become my best friend. I wondered if the teachers wouldn't like me, but never did I think I would find myself in this situation.

What was I supposed to do?

Who was I to turn to?

How could I get them off my back?

I replayed the scene from the classroom, then on to the portacabin where I met the other girls. I shuddered when I thought what might have happened to me if Tia hadn't turned up.

Tia.

I thought about how, when I first met her at the bus stop, she seemed so fearless as she dragged me out of the way of the car. She saved me from harm. I tried to understand what she meant about being a Christian. I had never heard a 'Christian' talk the way Tia did about God and how he lives in her and helps her in all she does. She seemed so passionate about him. It was weird to me, but at the same time I sort of envied her strong faith. It must be so reassuring to know that some sort of high power or person was looking out for you, day and night, and on top of that you were given inner peace and strength.

I could do with some of that right now!

Silent tears slid down my face and plopped onto Roly's brown curly fur. I'd heard about people being bullied before. I had imagined that if it ever happened to me (which seemed so remote at the time), I would stand up for myself, I would fight back. I wasn't a coward, and people just couldn't push me around and reduce me to tears – until now.

What was so different now?

Marshton Hills.

My head was pounding. Sleep drifted into my troubled mind and carried me far away.

Lois, Lois. Long green leaves with sharp tips scratched my skin as I ran. My legs were aching, but I couldn't stop. A whispery voice kept calling my name, but I couldn't see who it was. Measured footsteps were behind me, getting closer and closer. The trees were pressing in on me. The heat was oppressive and the darkness was tangible. I tried to run faster, but the leaves were like hands and were grabbing my shoulders. I was suffocating. 'Somebody help me!' I screamed. 'Help, help, help…'

I sat up in bed. My body was drenched in sweat. Roly had fallen out of bed, and I bent over to pick him up. Rubbing my face, I realised that I had had a bad dream. I can't remember the last time I had had one. I knew that Carmel and her threats had brought it on. Anyone could have figured that out. I decided to have a shower. Maybe freshening up might clear my head and help me to think. Opening my door, I heard voices. Loud voices.

'I have to pay it Ron, and now.'

'What now?' shouted Dad. 'You are supposed to be earning money, not spending the little that we've saved for emergencies, you stupid woman.'

'How dare you call me stupid!' screamed Mum. 'You're the greedy one. We wouldn't be in this position if you hadn't wanted more. More shops, more money, more of everything. You're a fool, Ronald, a selfish, greedy fool!'

I heard a crash.

'Yes, that's right,' bellowed Dad, 'blame me. But who was I doing it for, eh? You wanted a new car every year, holidays, private schools for the girls. You wanted to laze around all day long, doing your nails, you—'

Something heavy fell to the floor. I stepped back quickly into my room. My mind was racing. I have never heard my parents scream and shout at each other like that before. They were usually loving and considerate towards each other. This was the effect that Marshton Hills was having on them.

I walked over to the window. The greyness outside had turned black. It was hard to distinguish the cars and the facing wall and the junk from each other. It was just a mess.

Was this how our lives were going to be?

* * *

The pale morning sun filtered through the gap in the curtains. Groggily, I turned over and looked at my bedside digital clock – 07.31. I had spent the whole evening in my bedroom. I'd waited for either of my parents to come up and see me, but they hadn't. Hunger pangs cramped my stomach. I hadn't eaten all day, but even now the thought of food was sickening. Last night was rough. I had tossed and turned for so long, I was surprised that there wasn't a big hole in the middle of the bed!

My school uniform hung on the wardrobe door. It repulsed me, and I wished that I could wear a pair of jeans and a T-shirt and slope off for the day. I didn't know where or what I would do, but not going to school would be a big help.

Downstairs, the wrecked kitchen shocked me.

'Morning, Lois,' said Mum, throwing broken crockery into a box.

One of the chairs was missing a leg. Mum's hair was standing up on end and her eyes were red. Our eyes locked. Mum continued to pick up the pieces. For that split second I wished that she would hug me and then we both could have had a good old cry. I would have told her about school then. It was too late now. It felt like there was a barrier between us. Silently I helped Mum to tidy up. I wanted to say so much, but I couldn't. For Mum and Dad to have been reduced to fighting and quarrelling, things had to be bad.

'Morning, Lois,' said Dad. He didn't even look at Mum. Dad made himself some coffee and walked out.

A thought hit me. 'Mum, are you and Dad getting divorced?'

'Don't be silly, we've just had a disagreement, that's all.'

'A disagreement. It looks like a lot more than that. How about a major big bust up?'

Wearily, Mum said, 'Lois, I'm very tired, why don't you just get yourself off to school. We'll have a good chat tonight, okay?'

Mum's words stung me. Usually we would have had a chat there and then to clear the air. But then again, nothing was usual at the moment. It's not usual for my parents to fight and argue. It's not usual for Mum to have no time for us to have a heart to heart. I hoped that things would change soon – but I wasn't holding my breath.

I decided to walk to school. I hoped I would arrive late, and the gates would be locked so that I wouldn't be able to get in. Wishful thinking. My legs felt like lead and each step was an effort. If there was somewhere that I could hide myself away all day, that would be where I would be going now.

But there wasn't.

The school gates loomed up in front of me all too quickly. Most pupils were making their way towards the main entrance. I wished now that I had taken Tia's phone number when she had offered it. But I honestly thought that I would have made at least one new friend in my class. Now it seemed like I was marooned on an island surrounded by this vast sea of strangers. I scanned the faces for Tia, but she was nowhere around. At the main door I was just about to step into school when someone called my name.

'Lois, Lois!'

I looked behind me and saw a couple of faces that I recognised from my class. Tentatively, I stopped and waited for them to catch up with me. One of the girls was black and the other white. They were smiling.

'Hi,' said the black girl. 'I'm Anita and this is Gemma. We saw you on your own so we thought we'd keep you company.'

I was wary of them as they got on either side of me. It was only yesterday that Jennifer and Neera did likewise, and the end result was far from pleasant.

We walked, or rather they bounced along and I walked, to registration together. By the time we settled into our first class of the day, I felt a lot better about school. Jennifer and Neera hadn't turned up, and my new friends seemed genuine and fun to be with. They were like a double act; one would say something and the other one would respond with a laugh or a complaint or something, but I sensed that they were good friends. I was glad that they seemed to want to be my friend. I wanted to tell them about Jennifer, Neera and Carmel, but not yet. I thought that once I got to know them better, perhaps I would.

At break-time they asked me if I wanted to have a drink or something. Memories of my last encounter at break-time loomed in my mind. My mouth was dry and I tried to swallow. I was stalling. I wasn't sure what to do. 'It's okay if you don't want to,' said Anita.

'No, eh, it's alright, I'll come with you.'

They led me to the canteen. I just brought a drink, but both girls brought two bags of crisps each and a can of Coke, and some sweets.

'This will keep us going until lunchtime,' scoffed Gemma.

'Hey, why don't you come with us at lunchtime?' asked Anita. She looked away from me as she spoke.

'Okay,' I nodded. It was a nice feeling that I wasn't left on my own. I was warming to these girls more and more. Although, Anita seemed a bit sad, but Gemma was quite sparky.

'Maybe we could go to the chip shop. Or there's a nice bakery round the corner, it's clean and their doughnuts are wicked,' confided Anita, who seemed a bit more cheerful as she mentioned food.

'No, no. Let's have kebabs. I love kebabs,' grinned Gemma.

'Kebabs? You're joking. That meat could've been on the skewer for weeks. Didn't you see that programme on the box the other night? "Worse Café in London" or something like that it was called. It was terrible. The man said that kebabs are a breeding ground for bacteria. Forget kebabs,' warned Anita.

'But I love them – all that meat, it tastes so juicy,' Gemma said licking her lips. 'It must be all those germs.'

I laughed at them. They were really funny. Smiling and feeling much lighter than I had for days, I told them that I didn't care what we had.

'Right, we'll decide when we get out of school,' said Gemma.

The morning flew by. Maths isn't my favourite subject, but Mr Preston was strict, and the class was under his control throughout the lesson. Afterwards, outside the school gates, Anita and Gemma appeared to be undecided on what to do for lunch.

'I'll tell you what, why don't we go to my house for lunch,' offered Anita. 'We can have whatever we find in the fridge or cupboards. No one's home, we can relax for a while. What do you say?'

'Yes!' shouted Gemma. She looked at me and said, 'Anita is a brilliant cook, you'll love her food.'

That settled it then.

'How long will it take to get to yours?' I asked Anita.

'Not too long,' she said.

* * *

We were sitting on the top deck of a bus watching Marshton Hills go by. Anita and Gemma were sitting in front of me and were strangely silent. Sitting behind them, I was beginning to feel uneasy, but I put that down to my bad experience with Carmel. I must admit that I was wondering why Anita wanted to go home when we only had an hour for lunch. It was taking well over fifteen minutes just to get there. We would have to eat really quickly and then head back to school.

Still, I reasoned, at least I now had two friends, which is more than I had yesterday.

Getting off the bus, Anita and Gemma's conversation became more animated as we quickly walked towards a large housing estate. Washing was hanging out from balconies. Scruffy, grubby young children were running about all over the place unsupervised. The sun was trying its hardest to break through the clouds, but it wouldn't have made any difference to this estate. The bleak greyness of the flats reached up towards the sky. Everything was infected with it. I felt a bit claustrophobic as we made our way deeper into the heart of the estate. It was like a jungle.

'Watcha, Nita!' shouted a little boy.

'Alright Harry, how comes you're not at school?'

'You know how it goes.' He laughed.

Gemma linked her arm through Anita's as they purposefully walked towards Anita's home.

Or so I thought.

They stopped abruptly outside a ground floor maisonette and knocked on the door.

Panic seized me. 'Anita, why are you knocking? Isn't this your house?'

'No, it isn't.' She turned to face me, and she looked sad. 'I'm sorry, Lois, but we had to bring you to Carmel's place, and this was the only way that we could think of to get you here.' Gemma stepped back and stood behind me.

'There was no way I was going to get myself beaten up for *you*.' Gemma pointed her finger in my face.

The front door opened. 'About time too,' said Jennifer with a smirk on her face.

6

'Hi, Lois,' said Jennifer, as she leapt out the door and grabbed my arm. Anita and Gemma stepped back just in time. Neera appeared and quickly grabbed my other arm. Momentarily, my mind was numbed. I think I was more shocked that Anita and Gemma had befriended me only to lead me into a trap than I was to see Jennifer and Neera. It was too late for me to make a break for it. Crossing the threshold of the flat I looked with pleading eyes at Anita and Gemma. Anita looked away, but Gemma stared back. Her look was one of indifference.

'Why?' I croaked.

Gemma shrugged. 'I told you, and anyway, it happens to us all.'

The door closed behind me as I was frog marched deep into the flat. I didn't have to wonder for long whose place it was.

Carmel had a cigarette in her mouth and a mobile phone against her ear. She was reclining in a leather chair with her feet up. Neera sat down on the floor and started to sort through some clothes. Surprisingly, the flat was very neat and tidy, although the ceiling and walls had a yellow tinge to them. Smoke. The living room was dominated by a green three-piece, leather suite, with matching pouffe. Without stopping her conversation, Carmel indicated with a nod of her head for me to sit down. Tentatively, I perched on the edge of one of the armchairs. Jennifer and Gemma both casually lit up cigarettes and sat on the settee. Ellie came into the room and she was in her nightie.

'Oh, we have company I see,' she laughed.

Nobody responded.

The doorbell rang and Ellie went to answer it. I couldn't move. I didn't know what was going to happen and I couldn't stop my mind leaping and jumping through all different kinds of scenarios.

Was I going to be beaten up? Would they take all my money? Not that I had very much.

I wished that I had the guts to run out the door. But I was too frightened. Besides, I didn't think that they would let me out. I kept asking myself why I hadn't realised that Anita and Gemma had set me up. There had been nothing that was obvious to me in their behaviour to give me the finest clue. I wished I had put up a struggle, and fought and kicked at Jennifer and Neera instead of meekly allowing them to bring me into the flat. Carmel waved her hand at Anita, who was leaning against the doorframe, to come into the room. Anita plonked herself down on the settee and folded her arms. She seemed really uncomfortable. I looked at her. She looked back at me, and if eyes could speak, I felt that she might have said she was sorry. But it was a bit too late for that now.

Then I had a horrible thought: nobody knew where I was. It had taken over half an hour to get to Carmel's house. I realised then that these girls had no intention of going back to school for the afternoon. I have no real allegiance to school, but I sure would have preferred to be there than here. Besides, I'd never missed school unless I had been really ill, so this was a first for me and I didn't like it. I wondered what the school would do about truancy. Did they contact your parents? How often did you have to be absent from school before they began to investigate?

I could hear voices in the hallway. The living room door was pushed open wider and a group of young people came in. Fear took hold of me again in a fresh wave, and I sat back in the armchair, eyes glued to the carpet. I tried to act invisible. It didn't work.

'Who's she?' a male voice said.

Carmel was off the phone by now and replied, 'Lois. She's recently moved here, and she's already found herself a fantastic job in "Go Sports", that new sports shop in Pattison Road.'

The young guy came and perched himself on one of the arms of the armchair that I was sitting in.

'Whassup? My name's Beriah Ansah, but my mates call me Beri. Nice to check yer.' His voice was pleasant, and he sounded very sure of himself.

I looked up and saw a handsome, appealing face. His burnt oak-colour skin glowed, and was smooth as though it had been polished to a high sheen. He was probably about seventeen or eighteen, but something in his eyes and the way he held himself made me think that he might even be older.

'Hello.'

'So, you work in a sports shop, then?'

I nodded.

'That's good.'

'She can get us—' Carmel was cut off in mid-flow as Beri raised his hand. I was really impressed by his obvious authority over her. I sat up a little straighter. If this guy could silence Carmel just by holding up his hand, he had my approval. My heart soared, and for the first time in the last couple of days I felt a little like my old self.

'You girls get yourselves sorted. Lois and I are going to get something to eat, okay.'

There was a lull of activity as all eyes were on me, and then everyone seemed to move at once. I caught the look that Carmel gave Beri before she turned and left the room too.

'Lois, where would you like to go?'

I was amazed at how Beri seemed to have such command over everyone. No one questioned him or argued with him. He spoke, they responded.

I looked at my watch and said, 'School. I'll probably be a little late, but I would rather be late than not go at all.'

'Okay, c'mon then, I'll go back as far as the school gates with you.'

And he did.

Beri's burnt gold-coloured Fiat Punto convertible car further impressed me. I wondered how he was able to afford it, but I pushed the thought right out of my mind. On the way to school, we chatted as though we had known each other all our lives. He was very good company. He told me that he had already left school, and was going to a college in Stadley to do graphic design.

'My uncle owns a garment factory, and I help with his designs and cutting.' He smiled at me, with one hand on the steering wheel and the other casually draped across the back of my seat.

'How on earth do you know somebody like Carmel?' I asked. My face was screwed up in puzzlement. I wondered how Beri, who seemed such a nice, cool guy, could associate himself with someone like her.

'She's family.' His laugh was like music to my ears. With each turn of the car's wheel, I liked him more and more.

'Is she your cousin?'

'No, not really. But our families go back in time, you know. Poor Carmel.' He shook his head.

'Poor would not be a word I would associate with Carmel.'

'I don't mean poor in money, but life. She's had a rough ride. Her dad was evil, man, I'm telling you. All he did was beat up and thump down. Her mum nearly died after he finished with her one night. How the police never locked him up is a mystery. There's a lot going on in her life right now, so go easy on her.'

'Go easy on her!' I shouted. 'What about me?'

'You're cool, baby.' He stroked the back of my neck. 'You're sweet, too.'

I grinned. Angry thoughts about Carmel seemed to float away.

The sun's rays were warm. I felt like I was melting. Everything so far about Beri was really nice. There was so much about him that seemed good. His appearance, his manner, his personality... I couldn't fault him. He stopped outside the school gates and asked me for my phone number. I hesitated for a moment and he said, 'No problem, if you don't want to give it to me, that's fine.'

'No, no, here it is.' I hastily scribbled down my mobile number on some paper I tore out of my folder.

I have only ever given my phone number to one guy – Russell – who was interested in me. We went on a few dates, until I realised that he just wanted to meet my dad who was a known cricket fanatic in Hartenswood, and so was Russell!

Beri flashed his white teeth at me and I thought for a moment that he was going to kiss me. Instead, he squeezed my fingers. 'Catch you later, right.' He was still holding my hand. Neither of us wanted to break the contact. Finally he lessened the hold on my hand, and I hastily put my hand in my pocket and climbed out of the car.

'Lois, Lois!' I turned in time to see Tia, breaking out from a group of girls and charging up to us like a mad bull. She stalked up to me and grabbed my arm. 'What are you doing with him?' She jutted her chin in Beri's direction and wrinkled her nose as though she had smelt something unpleasant. The girls that Tia had been with stood and watched from a distance.

He grinned at her. I was fuming. Shrugging Tia off my arm I said, 'What's it to do with you?' I took a step closer to the car. As far as I was concerned, Beri was my knight in shining armour. Even though Tia had rescued me before, she didn't own me.

'What is it to do with me?' she pointed to herself. 'Well, apart from the fact that I know what he's about – he's a total criminal and he's a manipulator and a soul thief.'

Beri laughed out loud and so did I.

'A soul thief?' I said, incredulous. 'Are you for real, Tia?'

Tia's mouth was pursed up tight like she was sucking lemons. Her eyes bore into Beri's smiling face.

Turning to one side, with his finger pointing at Tia, Beri looked at me and said, 'You see this girl, we once could've had a thing going, but she turned all religious and because I wasn't interested, she became my enemy.'

'You haven't changed one bit Beri, have you? Tell the truth, go on speak the truth for once in your life.' Tia looked at me and said, 'Okay, Lois, you're a big girl, right. If you want to believe everything this liar tells you, there's nothing I can do. But I'm warning you that nothing, absolutely nothing, but aggravation will come to you. If you think Carmel is a problem, you haven't seen nothing yet.' She took one long look at Beri and stormed off. She marched up to her friends and they walked off together. One of them turned and looked at me and Beri. He laughed and waved at her. She turned away.

I was shaken. Tia sounded so convincing and I guess I began to wonder whether I'd seen Beri through an adrenalin haze. I looked at Beri and his eyes were like melting chocolate, smooth and irre- sistible. His smile soothed away the confusion that Tia's words had caused. How could this guy be wicked? He certainly didn't look it. In fact, he generated security and warmth. I decided there and then that I would trust him.

'Lois. I want to be truthful with you. I used to like Tia very, very much. We were really good friends. And I won't lie and say if she hadn't become a holy roller, we could have had a nice time. As you can see, she's become bitter and twisted. Shame, you know, she was nice girl.'

I looked Beri deep in the eyes. I was trying to sort

out what Tia had said, and what Beri was saying. I couldn't help but believe Beri. Tia had burst in on us, ranting and raving. I remembered that she had spent ages telling me about her Christian experience, and it sort of reinforced what Beri was saying. Maybe she was bitter now?

'Look, sweetness, I have to run. I'll give you a ring tonight, okay?' He looked at me as if to ask my permission.

Nodding, I said, 'Yes, yes, that will be fine.'

I began to walk towards the main building. Beri called out, 'You speak nice, Lois, don't lose it.'

I felt embarrassed and grinned, giving him a little wave. I floated towards school and when I got to the door, I looked back and saw Beri's car still in the same place. He was watching me. It gave me a warm feeling. I turned to wave to him as I was walking through the door: he was still there. Sighing with deep pleasure I walked along the corridor. I had missed registration and I didn't feel like going to my class, but I did. It was double geography. Throughout the lesson I was lost in a wonderful daydream about Beri. I felt good too, because Jennifer and Neera were absent. I thought about how Beri handled Carmel, and I think, if I'm being honest, that was the thing that had attracted me to him. It was such a relief that he'd got her off my back. I realised that if I could keep on the right side of Beri, that might keep Carmel away from me. I was so amazed that Carmel was like a lamb in Beri's presence. The change was incredible.

My mind was made up. I had to stick to Beri at all costs.

The class ended and I was making my way out of

the door when someone tapped on my shoulder. It was a short white girl. She was wearing the thickest glasses I have ever seen, and her teeth were a mangle of metal.

'Hello, you're the new girl, aren't you?'

'Yes, that's right. Why do you want to know?' My voice was hostile. I wasn't about to trust anyone again – apart from Beri.

Nervously, she stammered, 'Oh, oh, I just wanted to say hello.' It dawned on me then that she was a loner and was looking for a friend. She must be really desperate.

Feeling a bit sorry for her, I introduced myself. 'I'm Lois, what's your name?'

'Samantha. Can I walk with you?'

'Sure.'

She began to chat non-stop. Throughout her incessant chattering, I detected that 'Sam', as she liked to be called, hadn't made any close friendships since she had been at the school. Nobody wanted to mix with her. I'm not sure that I did either. By the time we reached my bus stop, I had had enough of her.

'Shall we swap phone numbers and ring each other up tonight?' Sam was quick to dig out a piece of paper and a pen and push it under my nose. I looked at her. She was definitely not the sort of girl I would like to hang around with. She didn't look too good, her dress sense was rubbish, and I just knew that if I took her on as a friend, she would cling to me tighter than moss on green slimy rock!

'Eh,' I said evasively, 'I can't remember my mobile number just now, maybe I'll remember it tomorrow.'

'Oh.' A light came on in her head. She sussed then

that I wasn't too interested in her. It made me feel a bit bad. I was just going to offer her my home number when I felt someone grab me by the scruff of the neck.

'Get lost, frog eyes.' It was Carmel, her unmistakable voice cutting through my new-found confidence.

Sam scuttled off like a rabbit and my buoyant mood left me.

Carmel half dragged me along the road away from the bus stop. When she let me go, I looked around and saw her three sidekicks, Ellie, Jennifer and Neera, all smoking. I was trapped.

'Keep walking,' hissed Carmel. With leaden feet, I slowly walked with them. Away from the bus stop. Away from school. Away from safety. Carmel was chewing my ear continuously.

'…You're not here for a day and already you've wormed your way into Beri's affections. You sussed that the guy is soft on girls. And you,' she prodded me, 'you homed in like a bee to honey.'

'But, but, I don't want him like that.' Any thoughts I had about Beri and I being an item were quickly dashed. No way did I want that guy if I had to pay for him with more trouble from Carmel. Unless… unless he could keep her away from me. But could he?

'Well, girl, I'm telling you now that if you thought I hated you before, now you have perfected that hatred beyond belief.'

I would've loved to have asked Carmel why she hated me. She hardly knew me, but it was obvious that something about me was totally abhorrent to her. I sensed her hatred the first time I had met her in the portacabin, and now she had confirmed it. But why?

'Beri is my guy,' she whispered softly into my ear. 'And I aim to keep it like that.'

Sweat ran in rivulets down my back. Every step was an effort. I didn't dare turn to the left or right. Anyway, I wouldn't have received any support from her mates. They moved together as one solid unit, like a python that surrounds its prey and slowly crushes it to death. I wished that I had taken Beri's phone number. I couldn't wait to get home and wait for his call so I could tell him about Carmel and her craziness. I wanted her permanently off my back, and as far was I was concerned he would be the one to do it.

'Okay,' said Carmel. She sounded less angry. I was sure that she could hear my heartbeat thundering in my throat.

'I have a plan. Let's get to the sports shop. You're going to help us. And I know you won't say no.'

7

'Right, this is what I want you to do.'

She outlined her plan and I was convinced then that she was completely and utterly mad.

Carmel was prepping me on the corner of my road. Her voice was droning on and on. The others were adding words of encouragement to whatever she was saying. I sort of switched off. What was happening to me seemed so surreal. Six months ago I was living such a different life that this still felt like a bad dream.

I had realised from my first contact with Carmel not to say too much back to her. I think my voice spiked her up. But now she was prodding me with her finger. 'Did you hear me, Lois, did you hear?'

Her plan made me want to laugh. I was on the borderline of manic hysteria. But I couldn't, or more accurately wouldn't laugh, as I was too scared of the consequences. I pinched myself to stop the crazy laughter from bubbling out of my mouth, but at the same time I wanted to cry. People were walking past us on the other side of the road, and driving their cars, going about their business, not taking the slightest notice of a group of schoolgirls on the street corner. I wondered what would've happened if I had shouted out for someone to help me. Would I be rescued from Carmel and co? Probably not. I couldn't see anyone wanting to get involved.

'C'mon, let's go.'

Silently, I followed them. Carmel's plan, which she had obviously thought out, appeared to be so simple and straightforward to her, but was a nightmare for me. She'd come up with the idea of me stealing stock from my dad. Of course, she didn't know he was my dad. I let her believe the assumption that he was just my boss. But she had thought that it would be easier for me to steal the trainers than for her and her friends to steal them. Nice.

How in the world did she think that I was going to give her a boxed pair of trainers without my dad seeing the exchange between us? And, furthermore, even if he didn't see it, surely when he did stock-taking he would realise that a pair was missing?

My breathing was coming in short, sharp spurts. My head was spinning as we approached the shop. I was desperate for a way out. My steps were faltering as I tried to delay the whole sorry scenario.

We were one shop away when the door of the sports shop opened. Out stepped Niecy.

'Oh, Lois, there you are.' She rushed out and hugged me. Holding me at arms' length she said, 'Are you alright?' She looked at Carmel and the others. 'Are these your friends? Hi.' She smiled at them. Ellie, Jennifer and Neera said hi back, but Carmel just glared at her.

I was rooted to the spot and my mouth was hanging open. 'Niecy,' was all that I could muster. I had been hoping and praying for a way out. This was perfect!

'Well, don't just stand out here, come into the shop.' Niecy stepped back into the shop and held the door open for us. My fingers were crossed. I was wishing hard that they would decline. But they didn't. Jennifer went first and then, one after the other, they stepped into the shop, with Carmel at the rear. Mum was sitting at the counter writing out labels. Dad was nowhere to be seen. Mum stood up as we congregated just inside the shop.

'Come in, girls. It's so nice to see that Lois has made some friends. Would you like a drink, or something to eat?'

Nobody responded at first then Ellie said, 'Yes thanks, I'll have whatever's going.' She sat down and the others followed.

For the next fifteen minutes, I was struck dumb with shock at the ease in which the girls and my sister were chatting. Mum had disappeared upstairs, and I wanted to join her, but I also didn't want to miss out on anything that would be said in my absence.

Carmel stood up first. 'Well, nice to have met you eh, Netty?'

My sister laughed. 'No, Niecy, short for Eunice. You must call again.'

'Oh yeah, we will. C'mon girls,' said Carmel. Like a sheep dog, she herded them out of the door. Carmel turned and with a slight nod, ordered me out of the door. I went at her beckoning.

Closing the door behind me, I gritted my teeth and followed them around the corner. My back was against the wall, and they surrounded me.

'Sister, Mum, Dad?' Carmel smiled, counting out each name with her fingers. 'Family business, that's good.' She bent her head towards me and snarled, 'How long did you think you could keep that bit of information to yourself, eh?' Her penetrative stare was hard and the spite that was emanating from her was scaring me.

'This changes the picture completely. I think Beri will be very interested in this bit of news.' She looked at me and smiled with her lips, but her eyes were vindictive.

My bladder was threatening to empty itself, and my knees were about to give way. I felt so weak and helpless. It was a hard job to keep back the tears that were just one breath away from overspill.

They stood around me, not speaking just staring, for what seemed like an aeon, but was in fact only a few seconds. I didn't even realise that I was holding my breath until they walked off. It took a while for me to gather myself together. I felt as though I had been brutalised, even though I hadn't been physically damaged. I stood still, watching the cars whizzing past. Everything was so unreal. Was this really happening to me or was I caught up in the worst living nightmare ever?

My feet felt as though they were fused to the pavement slab that I was standing on. If a policeman had walked by I wasn't sure if I would've been able to rush up to him and pour out my story. And would he have believed me? Would anybody believe me for that matter? Carmel and the others hadn't harmed my body in any way. It had all been words. I'd never imagined that words could be so powerful. Until they actually did something to physically hurt me, and I had the evidence to show like a broken arm or a bruise, I didn't think that there was anything I could do about those girls.

I thought about what my dad might say if I told him

that I was being threatened.

'Right. What's their names? Where do they live? If you can't tell me, I'll go straight to the Headmistress and *demand* that she take action. And if she can't sort it out, then it's a matter for the police.'

Mum would worry and hassle me for a moment-by-moment account and she would be at the school every minute, making the situation worse.

I wasn't sure what Niecy would say. At the moment she was so full of university life that she wasn't quite on this planet.

Feeling shattered, I dragged myself back to the shop. Mum was back at the counter writing her labels and I assumed that Niecy was upstairs.

Mum looked up as I came through the door. 'Hello, darling. Those girls were nice, are they in your class?' Mum's head was bent and she didn't see the shocked expression on my face.

'Nice, Mum?' I sighed. This ignorance from Mum sapped the last bit of energy that I had.

'Lois, I've got a job in a nursing home. I don't want to work there, but I haven't got much of a choice. At least I'll be able to save the money that I need to pay for a refresher course in nursing.' Mum had tears in her eyes, which she dabbed at with a tissue. 'It's just all so different,' she whispered.

The tears that I had been holding back escaped, and slowly flowed over my eyelids and down my cheeks.

'Lois, what have we come to?' Mum held out her hands, with her vivid red false nails. 'I have to have these clipped off tomorrow. My life is not my own anymore.' She paused and I could almost see the strong emotions going through her body. I watched Mum go through her own private struggle. What could I say to help her? How could I tell her about what I'd been going through? Looking at Mum I felt so helpless. So far, all that had occupied my mind was me. I hadn't given a thought to Mum, or anyone else for that matter. Living in this rabbit hutch was a complete reversal of life in Hartenswood. There, Mum was a member of the local exclusive sports club, and she went three or four times a week. She was a keen sportswoman and liked to keep herself fit. Since we had been in Marshton Hills, I had noticed that Mum had lost weight, but it wasn't due to any sports centre. I wasn't sure if there was one here anyway. That was the least of her worries.

Sniffing, Mum said, 'I suppose that my pride has been dented. I was so proud of what your dad had achieved. But he's lost it all and now we're reduced to this.'

We sat in silence, lost in our own worlds. There was no way that I could tell my mum the truth about Carmel. About school. About how I was hurting. About needing help. She was hurting herself.

Mum blew her nose. 'The truth is, Lois,' she dried her eyes, 'is that I have to thank God that as a family we are still together. When I really consider the things that we have lost, it's all material things that don't last long anyway.'

'Yeah, I suppose so, but it's nice not to have to count your pennies, isn't it?'

Niecy came into the room with a tray laden with a jug and glasses.

'Where have they all gone?'

To prison, I wanted to reply. If only that were true! That's where they should be.

Mum stood up. 'I've got a few things that I need to do.' She left us and went upstairs.

Niecy sat in her vacant chair. 'Mum's really taken this move badly. On the one hand, I can fully understand about the big house and all the trappings that we had in Hartenswood, but on the other, this,' she pointed her finger towards the window, 'this is real life. More people live on the breadline than how we used to live. I have a sense of belonging among these people. This is the pulse of the nation. Without these people of diverse cultures living together, this country would collapse.'

I looked at Niecy as though she had grown two heads. I stood up and took a step towards her.

'What are you talking about?' I moved closer to her, pushing my face nearer hers. 'You haven't got a clue, have you? When we lived in Hartenswood, you lapped up the lifestyle, even though you complained about everything. Our school, our house, the people there. Yet you weren't against spending the money that Dad earned. And what about the holidays and school trips abroad? The clothes, the cars we had? I didn't hear your voice of resistance against them. What's changed, Niecy?' I was shouting by now, tears running down my face.

'You don't even live here. You go to Kings' University, which is on the other side of town. Mum and Dad are paying for you to go, and you haven't even given a thought about how hard it is for them to keep you, or even about getting a job to help yourself. Well, have you?'

Niecy looked shocked. I didn't know whether it was because of my outburst or because I had mentioned about her getting a job. But I continued.

'You need to come down out of the clouds and get real.'

'Hold on a minute now,' Niecy retorted. 'Yes, I agree that I'm in a privileged position now to be at Kings', but I wasn't given the place. I had to earn it. And yes...' She paused, which made me think she had to think about what she said next. 'Yes, I have thought about getting a job, but Mum said not yet. Anyway, that's not the issue. What about your friends, do you think they will have a chance to make it to Kings' or any uni? You might, but I don't think they will. This type of neighbourhood keeps people locked in their place, and I—'

'Oh. shut up Niecy, you haven't got a clue about anything and especially not those girls.' My hands were clenched and I felt like hitting her. I thumped the counter instead. She jumped as though I had hit her.

'Those girls are evil, let *me* tell *you*. You want to know about those girls and how hard their lives are, well, they—'

The doorbell rang, cutting off my flow of words. Dad rushed into the shop wearing a big smile. 'Hi girls, keeping shop for me, where's your mum?' His words faltered as he quickly took in the situation.

'What's wrong?'

A large lump had clogged up my throat. My eyes and nose were streaming and I knew I looked a mess. I ran out of the shop.

'Lois, what's wrong?' I heard my dad call. Ignoring him, I ran into my room, slamming the door behind me. Throwing myself on the bed, I sobbed uncontrollably. I stuffed my duvet in my mouth. To be truthful, I didn't think that anyone would respond if they heard me anyway. Mum was completely wrapped up in her problems, Dad was absorbed with the running of the shop and no doubt Niecy would be filling his ears with her side of the story. And as for Niecy, she seemed to be caught up in some fairy tale life that was a million miles from reality. I wished that Dad hadn't come into the shop then, as I was just about to tell her about what my 'friends' were putting me through. She would probably have come up with some idea that they were 'a product of their environment'. So what? What about *me*?

The truth of the situation was that I had nobody. I had nothing. I couldn't help but feel sorry for myself.

There had to be a way in which I could defend myself – maybe it would be through Beri, maybe not.

But I had made up my mind that somehow I was going to survive.

8

The train pulled into Hartenswood at a minute past eight. It hadn't been too difficult to sneak out of the house so early in the morning. Mum was on early duty at the nursing home, so after I heard the front door shut, I had got myself ready and left.

Niecy had come up to my room just before she had gone back to university. I had pretended I was asleep, but she knew me too well.

'Lois, I want there to be peace between us. I know things are a bit difficult at the moment for you, but you're young, and you'll get used to life here.'

'Yeah,' was all I could muster. I had decided that it would be pointless to try and get Niecy to understand what I was going through. If I told her that I was being bullied, she'd probably just say, 'Those poor girls are living such hard lives, they can't help it.' I didn't need that.

She rattled on for about five minutes, and I let her. Usually, neither of us would have been able to get a word in edgeways, as we would have interrupted each other constantly. I sensed Niecy was a bit full of her 'university' self, and liked the sound of her own voice.

Kissing me on the cheek she said, 'You must come down and see me soon. I'll ring you.'

No doubt that would be when she'd torn herself away from her new-found friends and could spare half an hour for me!

Standing on Hartenswood station platform, the old familiar surroundings caused a deep sense of loss in me.

If only, if only...

Shaking my head, I made my way towards the exit. Once outside, I drank in the fresh morning air, which was much sweeter than Marshton Hills. The sky was clear and the day looked set to be a warm late summer one. A few girls walked pass me in the royal blue jacket, white blouse and navy blue skirt that identified them as Academy girls. Wistfully I wished I were still one, too. They chatted happily, carrying heavy bags, apparently eager to get to school. No one looked in my direction. I didn't expect them to, and anyway, the girls looked young – they'd probably just started in the autumn term.

I'd decided last night not to go to school today. I was still awake at midnight waiting for Beri to call me. He didn't. I tried to push the harsh words that Tia said to him out of my mind, but as the minutes ticked away, I began to believe them.

The way we had chatted in the car, I really thought that we had the beginnings of something special. I'm not an expert in relationships, but I think that I'm a good judge of people. I thought he was the real thing.

Was I wrong?

I had planned out what I wanted to tell him. I wanted to pour out my heart about Carmel and ask him to get her off my back. To hear him say that he would, that things would be alright, was what had kept my head together. Until midnight.

I'd tossed and turned all night long. I tried to imagine what could have stopped Beri from phoning me, but the different scenarios that leapt over one another in my mind were endless and confused me. I had to switch off. That was when I decided that there was no way that I was going to school. I wasn't going to subject myself to taunts or threats of any sort today. But where was I going to go instead?

Home, that's where. 'Home' to me was still Hartenswood. I wanted to phone Sophie to tell her that I'd be coming, but it was about four in the morning when the idea came to me. If I did go, I would have to leave early to catch the train. I thought that it would be best to phone her when I got near her house.

Walking through Hartenswood town centre, I wanted to throw my arms wide and sing and dance. Freedom! For the first time in days, I felt lighter inside.

Quickening my steps, I couldn't wait to see Sophie's look of surprise when she saw me. At the top of Sophie's road, I stopped and quickly called her mobile. Her answering service asked me to leave a message. 'Sophie, it's Lois. Call me now. It's urgent. I'm at the top of your road.' I stood looking at the phone in my hand, expecting Sophie to answer. No reply. I knew it was a bit silly of me to expect Sophie to ring me back, as her phone was switched off. But I could only hope.

I waited for a full ten minutes and then I took a deep breath and started to walk towards her house. I tried to keep as close as I could to the conifer trees and bushes that enclosed the large houses that I passed. I didn't want to meet up with Sophie's mum, Sally. I would have hidden myself in the masses of greenery if I did. I knew she would not have approved of my playing truant, whatever the reason. Sally would probably interrogate me, and call my mum. Then Sally, who's the unofficial editor of the Hartenswood grapevine, would have asked Mum what she was doing now, and a million and one other questions. Having Sally spreading it about that Mum was now working in a nursing home would be the last thing that Mum would want. When we had to move, Mum had embroidered the truth of what had happened to our family with some colourful threads of untruths. I had told Sophie the truth, but she knew what her mum was like and hadn't broken my confidence. I hoped.

The Saab Aero estate was parked in the circular drive – Sally's pride and joy. I scooted past it, ducking and half running round to the back of the large detached house. Peeking through the window, I saw a half-dressed Sophie stuffing toast – and she was alone. I tapped on the window.

'Sophie,' I hissed.

It was the window tapping that really got her attention. Startled, Sophie looked at me for a moment as though I was a space alien.

'Lois!' she mouthed, her eyes bulging with shock. With a finger over her lips, she indicated for me to go to the back door. Ever the drama queen, she tiptoed towards me. Opening the door she squealed, 'Lois, what on earth are you doing here?'

I was so pleased to see her that I threw my arms around her neck. 'I wanted to see a familiar face, so I took the day off school and came to see you.'

Sophie groaned. 'This is the very wrong day, Lois. We're off to on a field trip for three days to Norfolk.'

My buoyant mood was deflated like a hot air balloon falling out the sky. I had filled my mind with all the things I wanted to say to Sophie and the girls. I had stupidly imagined that they would spend part of the day with me. I bashed my forehead with my fist.

'Stupid, stupid, stupid,' I said between clenched teeth.

Sally bellowed, 'Sophie, come on!'

'Coming, Mum,' called Sophie over her shoulder. Looking back at me she said, 'Why don't you hide in the downstairs loo? Mum's in my room packing my bag. I'll knock on the door when it's clear for you to come to my room.'

'But what if she comes downstairs and wants to use the loo?' I asked.

Rolling her eyes, Sophie replied, 'You should know by now that Mum never uses the downstairs loo. It's for visitors only!'

I forgot that Sophie's mum was very fastidious, and she had a complete phobia about the thought of catching anything contagious.

'Okay then.'

I followed Sophie to the loo on tiptoes. She closed the door as I sat myself down. It was a large and airy room that could have doubled up as a spare bedroom! It seemed ages before Sophie came for me with a light tap at the door. With fingers on lips she beckoned me up the stairs to her room. Straight away, I could see it had been newly decorated. Gone was the pink colour scheme and in was everything yellow, cream and gold.

'Lois, I'll have to leave soon, so, tell me all your news quickly.'

I wondered where I should start, especially with such limited time.

'Sophie, are you ready yet?' called her mum.

'Coming!' shouted Sophie. 'Quick, Lois, tell me.'

Taking a deep breath, I plunged in. 'Firstly, I'm being bullied. Secondly, I've met a girl whose had an out-of-this-world religious experience, and thirdly I've met a guy who I thought we could become an item, but he's proven to be a bit unreliable. Plus I hate where I live, and as for the school, I—'

'Sophie!' roared her mum. 'We have precisely five minutes to get into the car and be outside the school. Now come on!'

Sophie quickly brushed her hair, applied some lip-gloss and sprayed some perfume on her neck, all in the space of a moment.

Throwing her arms around my neck she cooed, 'Oh, Lois, I miss you.'

I was so upset I nearly cried. I wished that I were going on the field trip to Norfolk. Six months ago, I probably would have been. Now I was an outsider to Sophie's life.

'Who is this guy? I want to know more,' said Sophie, ushering me out of her room.

Lacklustrely, I said, 'Beri. He's about eighteen and he's nice looking and—'

'Hmm, sweet,' smiled Sophie. 'Listen, Lois. I've got to go out the front door and get into the car with Mum. You'll have to slip out the back door at the same time, before Mum puts the house alarm on. It will go off if you leave it a fraction later, so get out quickly.' Sophie kissed my cheek.

'Come and see us soon, Lois. Preferably over a

weekend, you know how hard it is to miss even a few minutes from school. Okay now, bye.' She gushed down the stairs to be met by her irate mum.

I heard Sophie say, 'Mum, I need a quick sip of water.' Before her mum could answer, Sophie was back in the hallway, beckoning me down. I rushed down the stairs, and followed her into the kitchen.

'What's the problem?'

Sophie literally pushed me out the back door. 'I forgot that the alarm will go off if the back door isn't locked. Mum will know something's wrong – she's so fussy about locking doors and windows.'

'Sophie, come on!' blasted her mum.

'Quick!' said Sophie.

Leaping through the door, I crouched down and waited for a short while. I heard the car engine purr into action, then it was gone. So was Sophie. I sensed that our relationship had altered, drastically. The closeness had gone. Just a short while ago, Sophie and I were like Siamese twins. We did everything together. I still felt the same way about Sophie being my best friend. It was Sophie that had changed.

If I was honest with myself, I couldn't blame her. I had dropped out of her life like a leaf from a tree.

Looking at my watch it seemed as though the hands had hardly moved. Eight forty five.

What should I do now?

I reasoned with myself that I could go back to Marshton Hills and go to school. It would be easy to make up some lie about why I was late, but I couldn't bear the thought of going. Outside Sophie's house, I didn't know which way to turn. Then a thought occurred to me: why don't I go and see my old house?

With trepidation, I cautiously walked along the few streets between Sophie's house and my old home. I didn't quite know what I was going to do there, but I kept walking towards it. A young couple with two small children had bought it. Dad had had the most contact with them. Neither Mum nor I could bear the thought that these people would be taking over our house. I know it wasn't their fault, but I needed people to hang my anger, hurt and resentment on – and they fitted the bill.

I slowed down when I was one house away from it. Standing at the bottom of the circular drive, nostalgia overwhelmed me. The house still looked the same, although the net curtains, which had cost Mum the earth, had been replaced by blinds. The cars in the drive were different too, but the overall look of the house remained the same. My mood soared a few notches at the familiar sight. Then it seemed as though a mist enveloped me, numbing me and causing my eyes to go a bit muzzy. I felt drawn towards the house.

I bounced along the drive, happy and carefree. A surge of emotion welled up inside me and I laughed. 'Mum, I'm home,' I called. I danced round the side of the house. Where was everyone? I wondered. A child's swing was swaying to and fro in the garden, and a little white boy with fluffy, curly hair held on tightly and was giggling. An older girl was pushing him. But she stopped when she saw me. I stopped too. Who were they? I could hear a dog barking close by.

I shook my head, and my eyes seemed to get back into focus.

'Mum, Mum!' screamed the girl in panic. Then, looking at me she said, 'What do you want?'

'Nothing,' I stammered. 'I just wanted…'

Just outside of my vision, I saw a huge black dog bounding towards me. I turned to run, but the dog was quicker. He blocked my path and his ferocious barks and killer teeth stopped me in my tracks. I was petrified.

A woman charged out of the back door like a bullet fired from a gun. 'Hugo, Hugo, back now!' she shouted.

The dog stood still, snarling at me, black eyes intense, waiting for the order to impale its sharp, jagged incisors into my body. I stood like a statue, unblinking, unmovable. The woman lunged for the door, grabbing his collar. The dog resisted her tugging, but eventually it took a few steps back and stood with its owner.

'What do you want?' barked the woman.

My mouth was dry. Words that were in my brain could not form in my throat.

'Well, I'm waiting?' The woman had to use both hands to hold onto Hugo. The sight prompted my lips to start working. Words soon flowed.

'I, um, I used to live here and…' A lump in my throat blocked the rest of the words.

Instantly, the woman's attitude changed. 'Oh, I see. Yes, your face is sort of familiar.' She patted Hugo and said, 'Hold on a sec, I'll put him in the house.'

The woman turned towards the back door and led the dog away. The children were staring at me as though I had one eye in the middle of my head. I began to walk backwards. The woman was going to ask me a lot of embarrassing questions. I didn't want to answer any. When I got to the corner of the house I fled.

9

'Why didn't you stay and explain yourself?' asked Tia. 'I'm sure the woman would have understood.'

I shook my head. I couldn't explain to myself much less to some strange woman what I was going through.

The view through the coffee shop window was pleasant. The coffee shop was an annexe of Tia's church. The early autumn colours were soothing. Watching the birds fluttering about and pecking the ground for food took my mind off my problems until Tia wanted to know what had happened.

I had bumped into Tia outside Marshton Hills train station. My eyes were red and bleary – I felt sure I had cried enough tears to fill a two-litre Coke bottle. I was still a bit disorientated from my encounter with the new owner of my old house. On the journey home, I couldn't understand why I had decided to venture into the back garden. I suppose that the house had been mine for so long, reality fused with imagination and I sort of got confused. The scene played in my mind as I ran down the drive and up the road. I remember hanging over the rail of the little footbridge over the River Dalton. The river was flowing quickly downstream. I was alone. No one passed me either way. It had rained and I was soaked. It seemed so simple to hoist myself onto the railings. The river was beckoning me in. The ripples of water mesmerised me. I was swaying to the rhythmic sound. The battle of how I was going to get out of this mess was raging in my mind.

The move.

The bullying.

The rows between my parents.

The lack of any friends.

My new school.

The list was endless. But it was all adding up to one big rock-solid problem.

I wanted out.

Suddenly I was grabbed from behind and yanked back onto the bridge. A woman with long dangling earrings, a gold silk, appliqué patterned jacket and purple lipstick, and a little shaggy dog at her feet, was shouting at me. 'Are you on drugs? What are you doing hanging over the bridge? Do you want to kill yourself, girl?'

I thought that question would have been obvious. I didn't answer the woman. I only stared at her. She held onto my jacket.

'Well, aren't you going to say something?' Her voice was quite cultured and I guessed that she was probably some sort of arty person who had pots of money – to live around here she must have been well off.

I squinted at her as the rain came down relent lessly. As her grip loosened, I took off again.

'Hey, hey you!' she shouted. 'Whatever the prob lem is, killing yourself isn't worth it. I should know.'

I was gone.

'Lois, Lois, are you still with me?' Tia was waving her hand in front of my face. She was grinning at me.

A weak smile ghosted my lips in response. 'Yeah,

I'm here, just about.'

'This is painful, right?'

Nodding my head, I turned my face towards the window. I couldn't stop the tears falling.

'Listen, Lois, I don't know all of what you are experiencing, but I just want you to know that I'm here for you.' I knew that Tia was sincere, but I also knew that there was nothing that she could do to truly help me.

'I'm, I'm at a loss as to what I should do,' I gulped. It was difficult for me to take in air. 'What can I do? I can't fight them all, can I? I can't run away forever – where would I go? I've tried to work out why this is happening, but I can't find the answer. I'm not a bad person. I don't steal, or tell bad lies, I haven't hurt anyone, but this trouble has just landed on me like a great big dollop of low-flying bird poo! Why, why, why?' I bashed my head with my fist.

Grabbing my hand, Tia said, 'Don't do that you yourself.'

'Why not? If I don't, they will. That's what I'm dreading,' I whispered. 'Them beating me up.' Those words brought on a fresh bout of tears.

I felt a tissue being slipped into my hands. My head was almost touching the table as I dabbed at my eyes. The tears subsided, but the pain inside grew heavier.

'Hello, Tia,' boomed a voice.

I didn't bother to look up. I wasn't in the mood for introductions.

I heard Tia say, 'Hi Mabel, how you doing?'

'Fine, darlin', fine. Can I join yu?'

'I, eh…' Tia was obviously unsure whether or not I would mind.

'Yeah,' I croaked. I didn't want to stop Tia from

talking to her friends. I looked up and saw a plump black lady with a walking stick. When Tia had invited me along to the coffee bar at her church, she told me it was the OAPs' special day. Now I was meeting one of them.

'Hello, love, what's yur name?'

'Lois,' I said hoarsely.

'That's a nice name, biblical too. Yu live near here?'

'Yeah.' I didn't really want to talk to her, but I thought that being an old lady, it would be bad mannered not to.

'I haven't seen you in ages, Mabel,' said Tia.

'I been staying with my son and daughter-in-law.'

'Oh, that must've been nice for you.'

'No, it was terrible. My daughter-in-law don't like me.'

'Really?' said Tia.

'Yes, really. My son is torn between the two of us. I didn't want to go, but he insisted.'

'How did you manage to keep the peace?'

Mabel laughed. 'With great difficulty. Yu see, she don't do anything in the open. It's all under cover. She whisper something spiteful, and wait for me to explode openly. But, I don't. Well, most of the time I don't.' She smiled.

'What she don't realise is that I'm aware of her tricks. And 'sides, I have had a lot of experience of wicked people trying to bring me down.'

A slight glimmer of interest caused to me say, 'Have you? How did you deal with it?'

'Well, it was very hard at first. I come to England from Jamaica when I was just nineteen years old. I was so looking forward to starting life with my new husband. Imagine my shock that when we tried to get a place to live, the English people who rented the houses told us that they didn't want any monkeys in their houses. At work, people, other women, wouldn't talk to me. Openly they call me hurtful names, and ignore me. Things just went from bad to worse. Our windows were broke, people spat on us in the street, it was terrible. I wanted to go home to Jamaica, but I couldn't.'

'Why not?' Mabel's story had hooked me.

'Well, it cost a lot of money to sail back, and 'sides it would've been shameful to face everyone after we had told them that we were going to make our fortune in England. At that time *everyone* wanted to come to England. This was the mother country to us. English people come to Jamaica to recruit us as a workforce. We thought we would be welcomed with open arms. Huh, what a dream!' Mabel was smiling.

'So what did you do?'

'We took the insults and faced the rejection at first. But then the men, being men, began to retaliate. I was very angry too. I wanted to fight them all. Inside me,' she clutched her hand to her chest, 'a fire was raging. If I had been in a position to stab or shoot someone, I think I would've.'

'Really?'

Tia laughed and touched Mabel's hand. 'You, Mabel, killing someone? I don't believe you.'

'No, it's true, chile,' Mabel said earnestly. ' It's hard to understand why people hate yu for nothing more than the colour of yur skin, or something that yu might not even be aware of. The feelings that are churned up inside yu are so deep that they could drive yu to either kill others, or kill yourself.'

I knew what this woman was talking about. I also wondered whether Tia had orchestrated Mabel coming to talk to us, to me. Everything that she was saying was so close to the feelings I was experiencing. It was uncanny.

'So, what did you do?' I asked.

'I prayed.'

I felt deflated. I wanted to her say something spectacular like she gave someone a really good beating that frightened the others into leaving her alone, or something like that. But then I should have half expected that answer, seeing that we were sitting in a coffee shop in a church!

Mabel saw the look on my face. 'Listen, chile. Yu can't stop people from hating and abusing yu. Yu hate them back and see where it gets yu. I been a Christian from when I was your age. My grandmother taught me to trust Jesus. And I have to say he hasn't failed me yet. You know what happen to us then? My husband and some friends were so fed up with it all, that they decided to get together and buy a house. Bit by bit we all managed to scrimp and save to buy our own houses. After a few terrible years, the English people began to accept us. Not all, but some. Life just seemed to get better.'

'But it must have taken ages for things to change?'

'Yes, it did, but the greatest change was in me. And now, whenever I'm faced with difficult people, I just pray and let God be God. Things change in time, chile, things change in time.'

I could sense Tia's eyes on me. I didn't bother looking at her. What Mabel said was useless to me.

Praying was not the answer as far as I was concerned. If God was able to get Carmel off my back *now*, then maybe I would say that he was great. But I couldn't see that happening, and besides, why did he let it happen in the first place? This God business seemed a bit contrived to me. It was too easy to leave everything to 'prayer'. Surely you had to do something to help yourself, too.

Easing herself out of her chair, Mabel said her goodbyes and left us.

'Mabel's a character, isn't she?' said Tia.

'Yeah, I suppose so. I hope you're not going to start telling me about how wonderful Jesus is, though. I'm not interested.'

'No, I wasn't actually, except to say that Mabel has been through a lot in her life and she really knows what she's talking about. But I don't want to make it seem that what you're going through is trivial. It's just that whatever experiences we go through, all adds up to one thing.'

'Oh yeah, is that right? What's that, then?'

'It adds up to life. Everything we do, everything that happens to us, is part of life.'

'Well, my life at the moment is the pits. I just can't get over the fact that in a few days, my life has gone from good to terrible. Before Monday, I didn't even know Carmel existed. It's unbelievable.'

Tia looked as though she was going to say something. But she didn't.

'Tia, can I have a hand, please?' An ample sized lady with lovely light brown curly hair called her from behind the counter.

'Coming, Mum.'

'That's your mum?' I was surprised.

'Yeah,' smiled Tia, 'don't you think we look alike?'

They didn't. But I wasn't going to say so. Instead, I changed the subject. 'Why aren't you at school today?'

'Two of my teachers are off sick, and apparently the school couldn't get replacements, and I've got a free double period this afternoon anyway. So I was going to spend it in the library, but then I remembered that Mum had said that one of the workers for the coffee shop wouldn't be able to make it this morning. So here I am.'

She stood up and said, 'Do you want to help? It's only a bit of washing up and drying, but you don't have to.'

I had nothing else to do, so I said I'd help.

The kitchen was spotless. There were two old dears, Hattie and Sis, already in there, preparing lunch. They chatted and laughed non-stop.

'Hello, girlie,' said Hattie. She was a large black buxom woman with thick curly hair. I was shocked when, in scratching her head, she pushed her hair back – it was a wig. She roared with laughter at the expression on my face. Apparently, that trick was one of her specialities. The next couple of hours flew by as I helped with the waitressing. As the old people were getting ready to leave, Tia asked me if I would like to go home with her. I wasn't sure at first. The time I'd spent at the coffee shop had been great because I'd been able to block out the horrors of my life. But I didn't fancy spending time with Tia if she was going to bash me over the head with her religious beliefs. On the other hand, where was I going to go for the next two and a half hours? That would be the time that school finished. But then the choice was taken out of my hands. I was putting away some crockery when I heard Hattie and Sis say, 'Hell-oooo, Erica. You look sweet and nice. Come, give auntie a hug.'

I turned in time to see a tall, slim girl who looked like a model, with large brown eyes and shoulder-length black hair. She looked as though she had just stepped out of a film set. She wrapped her long arms around Hattie then Sis. Her light brown face shone, and her smile revealed white, perfectly even teeth.

Tia introduced us. 'Lois, meet Erica, my cousin from Canada.' She turned to her and said, 'Erica, this is Lois, a friend of mine.'

She smiled. 'Hi, nice to meet you, Lois.'

'Hi.' I smiled back. I just loved her accent.

'You coming back to our place, Erica? Lois is.'

'Yeah, of course I am. I've got some things to pick up. Do you want a ride, girls? I'm leaving now, though.'

'C'mon Lois, let's go.'

I didn't complain. I didn't even correct Tia at the time about why she didn't give me the chance of saying yes or no to coming to her house.

I think she'd guessed that I'd say yes!

10

Tia's living room had that lived-in feeling. A few magazines were dotted about the room, and a large bookcase ran from one end of a wall to the other. It was crammed with books.

'What do you think of England?' I asked Erica.

She grinned. 'I used to live here a long, long time ago. But it's cool.'

'How do you like it here in Marshton Hills?' Tia had told her in the car that I had recently moved into the area.

I wasn't able to answer her as her mobile phone rang. 'Excuse me for a moment,' she said, looking at me. I eased myself deeper into my armchair. For the first time in weeks, and since I had moved, I felt at peace with myself. The threats of Carmel seemed a million miles away.

'How are you feeling now, Lois? You seem a lot better,' said Tia.

I smiled at her, which was a first. 'Yeah, I feel more like my old self. Your house has a kind of homely atmosphere. It's calming.'

'Yeah, that's what most people say when they come here.'

I switched the subject onto Erica. 'Is your cousin a model? She looks like one.'

Tia laughed. 'Most people think that. It's probably because she's so tall.'

'She seems really calm and together.'

'Yeah, she is. Although, it's amazing really when you think of what she's been through.' I looked at Tia, willing her to go on.

She did.

Erica was the daughter of Tia's mum's sister, Paula. She met a Canadian guy and left England to go and live with him. No one really knows what happened, but she died in tragic circumstances when Erica was born. Erica was adopted by a Canadian couple and somehow she was able to trace Tia's nan in England. For the past four years she'd been visiting Tia's family.

'And do you know what? She became a Christian exactly three years to the day when I became one.'

'Oh.' What else could I say?

Tia seemed blown over by this fact – her eyes were sparkling, and she was grinning.

The doorbell rang. Tia jumped up and swung the door wide open. Two girls and a guy came into the house like the north wind. The girls pushed Tia onto the settee and began to pummel her with cushions.

The guy turned to me, grinning. 'Don't take no notice of them, they're so juvenile and—' A cushion landed on his head. He turned and joined in the rumble. By now it was on the floor.

Erica came back into the room and said, 'Gosh, you are such children!' Someone grabbed her ankle and she yelped.

It wasn't long before we were all rolling on the floor. How I got involved I don't know. But it was wild, and it was a great stress buster. I felt so much better. Erica, Cathy, Linda and Tom (I found out their names just before they left, they had only come to collect Erica) seemed like old friends, even though I had only just met them.

'Let's go up to my room,' said Tia as the front door closed on their goodbyes.

Her room needed a good going over. She hastily threw the duvet cover over the bed and straightened up the floor. I sat on her bed and watched her as she swept through the room like a tidal wave. Soon, Tia had her room looking half way decent. She pulled out a plastic tub from the bottom of her wardrobe. It was full of sweets.

'Help yourself.'

I did.

'I'm glad you're coming, Lois,' smiled Tia.

Tom had told me about some youth event that they were having at the church tomorrow night.

'It's gonna be fantastic,' Erica said.

'New Generation are a top group,' said Tom. 'You'll love 'em, Lois. Trust me.' He smiled.

I agreed to go simply because I couldn't believe that these young people, who were all Christians, seemed so normal and nice. These were the kind of people I would like to hang out with.

Tia switched on her CD player and music blared out of the speakers. I relaxed and thought that this was more like it. Tia didn't mention anything about God again. In fact, she was alright. We chatted about everything except for Carmel and school.

'Hi girls, you okay?' Tia's mum popped her head round the door.

'Fine thanks, Mum.'

'Would you like to have tea with us, Lois? I've

defrosted some chicken breasts and I thought I'd make a curry.'

They both looked at me.

I looked at my watch. Shaking my head I said, 'No, thanks. I'll have to be going soon.' If I didn't eat my tea at home, Mum would say that I should have told her I'd be out, as I knew that she would be expecting me to eat with her. Besides, she was on early duty today and to have to come home and cook, then not have the food eaten would get her riled. Mum's moods these days were unpredictable; sometimes she was like a raging bull, at other times she was so quiet and introspective that you forgot she was in the room. But when she was her old self, the house almost felt normal.

It wasn't long after that I was saying goodbye to Tia.

'Come again soon,' said her mum. I said that I would, as I felt that her mum meant it. Tia walked me to the bus stop. She linked her arms through mine and we strolled along like two old friends. She handed me a piece of paper. 'This is my mobile and home number. Anytime you need a chat or you want to come over, or anything, just give us a ring. Okay?' I took the paper and glanced at it quickly, then slipped it into my pocket. The bus came quickly and as I was about to step onto the platform, Tia pecked me on the cheek.

'Look after yourself girl, and I see you tomorrow.'

'Okay,' I smiled.

The bus pulled away from the kerb and drove off. I looked through the window. Tia was walking backwards slowly, waving at me. Smiling, I waved back.

I settled into my seat and thought about the day. It

had turned out good. I realised now that Tia *was* a nice person. Seeing her in action today with all the old people, I could tell by how she was with them that she genuinely cared. So, I reasoned to myself, she cared about me. Maybe what she had said about Beri was true after all. If *he* really cared about me, he at least would have phoned me. But he hadn't.

Thoughts about Carmel stabbed my brain like poisoned darts. What was I going to do about *her*? Tia had mentioned her a few times, but I had stopped her mid-flow. I didn't want the rest of my day to be spoiled with badness. It was too late, though. All day I had pushed the memories and pictures of Carmel and co out of my mind, but now those thoughts came back with a vengeance. I started to get so stressed about it that I ended up getting off the bus two stops before I should have.

I needed to walk, to think. Tia had said – quite a few times – that I should at least tell Mrs Crofton about what I was going through. But, I argued, what could she do about it? Tia said that knowing Mrs Crofton as she did, she would pull out all the stops, but that didn't answer my question. I knew there was nothing she could do.

As far as I could see, the only way out would be not to attend school. I had thought about asking my mum to get me a transfer, but what if Carmel and co found out which school I was at? And even worse, what if a new group of people decided to terrorise me there, too? No, I knew in my heart that the safest thing would be for me to stop going to school.

But what was I going to do, and where was I going to go?

Contemplating my situation, I was oblivious to what was happening around me. Suddenly, I felt a hand on my shoulder, and I screamed. As I spun round, my fear turned to relief. It was Beri. He threw his arms around me and planted a kiss on my forehead. Instinctively, I hugged him back. A wonderful warm feeling enveloped me, and my heart began to liquefy as I looked into his eyes. Then I remembered that he hadn't called me. I tried to pull away, but he held me fast.

Placing his fingers on my lips he said, 'I know, I know. I didn't call you yesterday because my mum was ill and I had to go to the hospital with her, okay?'

His words spun my mind around full circle.

'Oh Beri, I'm so sorry. What's wrong with her? How is she?'

'Hush baby.'

He brushed his soft lips with mine. Gently, he lead me to his car, which was on double yellow lines with the hazard lights flashing. He opened the passenger door for me, and closed it after I slipped into the front seat. His eyes slowly swept over me, drowning me in their intensity. Beri expertly nosed the car into the flow of traffic. I was just about to ask him where he was taking me when he said, 'You were going home, right?'

'Hmm, I was.'

'That's where I'm going to take you.'

I was pleased that he had said that. Even though I had got into his car quickly, I still wasn't feeling one hundred per cent sure about him. The car stopped a road away from the shop. Beri turned off the engine and turned to look at me.

'Lois, I've had a long talk with Carmel. You know something, people act or react to things that happen to them, and that girl is a prime example of that. She's had a bad life and she's now just living through the pain of it. She said to tell you that she's sorry that she freaked you out and came on too heavy. She wants to be your friend.'

Drawing back my head, I looked at him good, as though his nose had grown. 'You're joking. Tell me you're joking?'

He touched my hands lightly. With one eyebrow raised he said softly, 'I don't lie, do you hear me, Lois. I never lie.'

His words chilled me. It wasn't as though he raised his voice or gave me any indication that he was threatening me, yet, for a fleeting second, his words were laced with a hint of menace. He stroked my hand again, and his eyes looked so appealing that I wondered if I was imagining things.

'Carmel is a good and loyal friend, she's like a younger sister to me, that's why I said to you she was family. And to me she is. A lot of people misunderstand her, but she's cool you know.'

I found this a bit hard to believe. The Carmel who I knew was evil personified. There was nothing that I had experienced or seen that was cool. Neither was there any misunderstanding about her. In fact, it seemed very obvious to me the sort of person that she was. She had told me very clearly what she thought about me and what she was planning to do. How was it that her mind had now turned 180 degrees? I was suspicious. But I thought it best to keep my thoughts to myself.

'I'm glad she's changed.' I couldn't bring myself to say that Carmel had changed towards me, as I didn't know for sure if she had.

'She has, take my word for it. Anyway, let's talk about us, you and me.' Beri's stare bore through my brain and into my heart. This was all so new to me. Here was an older guy, with a car and lots of power and control, and he fancied me. Incredible. I didn't know how to behave or what to say that wouldn't show up my lack of experience. I wished there was someone who I could tell all my innermost fears and hopes to, especially about Beri, but there wasn't. I knew that Tia would be biased. I would just have to play everything by ear.

I wondered what I would do if Beri kissed me. I didn't have to wait long. His hand was on the top of the headrest on my car seat. He slipped it down until it was at the back of my head.

'Lois.' Beri said my name softly.

As I turned to look at him, he smiled at me and bent his head, and gently, as one would kiss a baby, I felt his lips touch mine. Beri's hand was now around my shoulders, and he drew us closer together. I was tingling right down to my toes. Slowly we drew apart. We sat staring at each other. There were so many questions that I wanted to ask him, like: why do you like me? What is it that attracts me to you? I wondered if the fact that he was black made it easier for me to be attracted to him. In Hartenswood, being the only black family for miles meant that the only boys I'd liked had been white. This was all so new to me.

'I want to ask you something, Lois.'

Beri's voice cut into my thoughts. My heart pumped faster and I wondered what he was going to say.

'I, eh, I...'

I held my breath and waited for him to speak.

He coughed and turned to look soulfully at me. 'Lois, I know this may seem a bit quick, but I would like you to be my girl. If you say no, I'll understand.'

I couldn't get the words out. Beri mistakenly thought I wasn't interested in his proposal.

'Okay.' He threw up his hands. 'You don't want to know. Fine. I can see that a fine, together, intelligent girl like you ain't gonna be too pleased to be seen out with me.' He started the car. The noise of the engine purring startled me into action. I grabbed his arm. 'No, Beri, I—'

He lightly touched my hand whilst looking in the rear view mirror. 'No problem. It's been nice knowing you, and I will—'

'Yes, Beri, I want to be your girl!' I shouted.

He looked at me with his mouth open. An incredulous look lit up his face.

'You mean it, you're not just saying this, right?' He turned his face slightly, and narrowed his eyes. I wondered how he would feel if he could look into me right at this moment.

For me, being his girlfriend would be the absolutely perfect way to keep Carmel off my back. And because Beri was a few years older than me, I felt protected and safe. The car and money were good things, too!

If Beri was able to keep Carmel away from me, it also meant that I could go to school if I wanted to. I wanted to soar out of the car window and high into the sky. I couldn't remember when I had last been so happy.

Beri clasped both my hands in his and kissed my nose.

'You're special you know, babes. Very special.' We sat looking at each other. The world outside seemed not to exist for us. My heart felt full and overflowing. It was all so weird at first for me.

Huskily Beri said, 'I'd better go now, before, before. Eh, look right, I come and pick you up after school tomorrow, okay?'

'Okay,' I whispered.

That settled it then. I would have to tell Tia that I couldn't make it to church. I had to admit to myself that I had only said yes because I liked Tia's cousin Erica and their friends. If Tia had invited me, I probably would have made some excuse not to go. Maybe I could go another time. Right now, Beri had asked me to be his girl, and I had accepted.

Hopefully this was the start of my new life.

My fingers were crossed.

11

I waltzed into the shop in a trance. Dad looked up expectantly. He must've thought I was a potential customer. When he saw it was only me, he grunted something and returned to the ledgers in front of him.

I was past caring. I was overwhelmed that Beri had asked me to be his girlfriend. I took the stairs two at a time. I was eager to speak to Sophie. Our relationship might have changed, but she was the only person that I could talk to about Beri. Tia wouldn't understand, and besides, she didn't like him.

Mum was cooking as I popped my head round the kitchen door. 'Hi, Mum.' I tried to quickly slip up to my room.

'Wait a minute, Lois,' said Mum as she turned towards me. I had no option but to go into the kitchen. I stood with my hand on the doorknob.

'Yes, Mum?'

'Well, come in, then. Sit down here, this is your home, you know.'

Dryly I said, 'How can I forget?'

Mum frowned. 'What's wrong?'

'Nothing.' My earlier euphoria at becoming Beri's girl had been replaced by the irritation and anger that was always under the surface.

Mum sat at the table and patted the chair next to her. I stomped into the kitchen and plonked myself down in the chair opposite her. I crossed my arms.

Mum looked at me for a minute, screwing up her face, as though she was trying to unravel a mystery. A mixture of emotions was bubbling up inside me, but I fought to keep it under control.

'Something bothering you?'

Counting on my fingers I reeled off, 'Marshton Hills, this flat, school, not having any money. Do you want me to carry on?' I looked expectantly at her.

Sighing, she said, 'I thought that since you had started school, you—'

I held up my hand. 'Don't tell me you thought that I had settled in nicely. Well, I—'

Dad burst into the kitchen. 'Lena, just look after the shop for a short while, I have to go to the wholesalers. Some new footwear has come in and I want the best of it first.'

Sighing, Mum said she would. Dragging herself up from the table she made her way to the door.

'Lois, we have to talk. I wanted to tell you that I'll be starting night duty soon, and you'll have to really help out with the cooking and cleaning and so on. For a start, you'd better sort out your room, oh, and the laundry needs to be done, too.'

'Are you joking, Mum? That's not my job,' I said indignantly. When we lived in Hartenswood, Maureen, our cleaning lady, used to come in twice a week and help Mum. 'Mum, you'll have to get a lady in to do the work. I'm sorry, but I'm not used to doing housework.'

'Well, it's about time you learnt.' Mum had raised her voice. 'You have got to stop thinking about Hartenswood, Lois. Those days have gone. Right now, I've got to work, and I can't do all the housework and cooking too. You'll have to work with me, not against me.'

'That's great.' My anger had bubbled over. 'I have to have my life interrupted so that you and Dad can get things together.' Pointing to myself I said, 'Was it me who took a gamble to get more money, and then lost the lot?' I was nearly screaming by now.

'Lois, don't talk like that. Your dad did what he thought best and—'

'And what? Is this the best he could do?' I spread my arms wide.

Tears were running down Mum's cheeks. I began to sob.

'I hate it here. I hate it so much. But what can I do, eh Mum? Where can I go? You can't begin to understand what I'm going through.'

'Oh Lord, what am I going to do?' Mum wept.

'You had better go and keep your eye on the shop, that's what,' I retorted. I ran out the door and into my room. I stood with my back against the door. I didn't want mum to come in. With my head in my hands, I cried. I knew that Mum was only trying to talk to me, but I'd turned it into a shouting match. I sensed that Mum wanted to talk about her new job, and how she didn't really want to do it, but that we needed the money.

But what about me? Now I was going to have to do housework and cook – no way. We'd have to have takeaways every night. There and then, I planned to be away from home as much as possible. I'd let Beri see to that. Just the thought of his name caused a thin shaft of light to shine through my darkness. The excitement that I had had when I first came home was rekindled. Wiping my eyes, I remembered that I was going to phone Sophie.

In the living room I sat next to the phone, composing myself. I wanted to tell Sophie about every feeling that I'd felt as Beri kissed me. I know that she would be very excited that I had agreed to be his girlfriend. Of my close friends, Sophie and Daisy had dated a few boys and Zara had been seeing her guy for two years. Lucy-Ann and I were the only ones that hadn't really dated. Until now!

Taking a few deep breaths, I held the handset and punched in Sophie's number.

'Hi, this is Lois, can I speak to Sophie, please?'

'She's away for a few days, Lois,' replied her mum.

'Oh no!' I remembered then that I had seen Sophie off on her field trip that morning. I slapped my forehead with the palm of my hand. How could I have forgotten? I had a short chat with her mum and replaced the handset.

I slumped in the chair. My mood plunged. Excitement was rapidly replaced with depression. Who could I confide in? Who could I even just spend some time chit-chatting with?

Maybe Beri would be that person – not just a boyfriend, but a good friend, too.

I sat up straight and began to replay in my mind the times when Beri and I had been alone. I decided that Beri was the answer to my problems.

* * *

I called Tia.

'Hi Lois, how are you?'

'Fine. I just wanted to let you know that I won't be coming tomorrow, I'm really sorry.'

Tia didn't say anything.

'Are you still there?'

'Yeah, yeah, I see. Why is that, has something important cropped up?'

I didn't want to tell her that I was meeting up with Beri, so I just said, 'That's right. Anyway, I've got to go. I'll speak to you soon.'

I hung up quickly. I felt a bit bad about letting Tia and her friends down, but not only did I want to go out with Beri, but there was the other matter of Carmel.

* * *

'Everyone enjoying the meal?' asked Mum.

Dad, Niecy and I all looked up from our plates and looked at Mum as though she had just spoken in Greek. Niecy was home for a few days.

What did she mean, were we enjoying the meal? It was just a meal. I looked closely at Mum. Was she feeling all right? She looked good. In fact, she looked radiant. She seemed calmer and more peaceful. I'd noticed, too, that life in the flat was a lot more harmonious. Mum and Dad spoke to each other without shouting and screaming. I was left to my own devices. I hardly did any housework, and nobody seemed to notice – which was great.

There were only two days left until Christmas. My fifteenth birthday was three days after Christmas, too. It's hard to believe that we've been living in Marshton Hills for over five months. The time has rushed by, and loads of things have been happening.

School has become a hit and miss affair for me. My attendance is erratic, and the school has sent letters home to my parents about my absences that, so far, I have managed to intercept. I remember when the first letter came. I was rifling through the batch of letters that the postman had just dropped through our letterbox. The school logo stood out on one envelope like a lighthouse beacon. Tearing it open quickly, I scanned the words and tore it up. I was petrified. From then on, I started checking the post to make sure no letters like that got through. I knew that I was being ultra deceitful, but the alternative was worse. The letter made me fearful of someone from the education authority knocking on our door. I started going to school a bit more often after that. But not for long! My attendance began to drop off after a while. I was hooked up on seeing Beri nearly every day.

The other thing was that I'd lost interest. The teachers were boring, so was the work. I'd seen Jennifer and Neera a few times, and I had bumped into Carmel. But, miracles of miracles, nothing had happened, except for a few dirty looks. That should have given me the confidence to return to school, but Beri had totally captivated me.

Everything took second place to him.

* * *

'I said, is the meal fine?' asked Mum again.

'Mum, it's lovely,' said Niecy, who started to go on about the different ingredients Mum had used. I didn't think that was what Mum had meant, but Niecy was sucking up to Mum because she wanted some money for Christmas.

Mum coughed and said, 'There's something I want to tell you all.'

Dad continued to tuck into his plate of fried fish with yam and green bananas. Friday night was fish night, and Dad's favourite meal of the week. He had the financial paper propped up in front of him. He was oblivious to Mum's announcement. She nudged him.

'Ron, I'm talking.'

He stopped eating and said, 'What is it?'

Mum cleared her throat again. 'I just wanted you all to know that I've become a Christian and I'm going to start going to church again.'

'Is that it?' scoffed Dad. 'I thought you were going to tell us that you'd been doing the Lottery on the quiet and that now you've hit the big time.'

Mum rolled her eyes. 'Money, money, money. Ron, are you ever going to think about something else, you know, something more important? Worrying over money is not good for you. It will kill you.'

'What do you mean that you've become a Christian, Mum? You always were as far as I'm concerned,' said Niecy, defusing the contention between our parents.

Smiling, Mum replied, 'That's just it. I was just going to church, but now, I'm going to church for the right reasons.'

'Which are?' said Dad.

Quietly, Mum said, 'You know, I really understand for the first time in my life what it means to have God's love.' A dreamy look came into her eyes. I had seen it before when someone had waxed lyrical about God – Tia.

'Lena, I hope you're not going to have an attack of religious mania. Life here would *really* become unbearable.'

'Well, let me tell you all something. For the last month, hasn't this house known peace? Hasn't there been some sort of unity? Well, let me tell you it's because I have prayed for these things, and God has answered. I'm learning that I need to have a close relationship with Jesus so that I can get through this period of our lives. I'm praying that you will all do the same.'

'Mum, you've got to be joking,' Niecy said. She wasn't smiling.

'I've never been more serious in my life, girl.'

Dad noisily finished his meal. Clanging the cutlery against the plate, he looked at Mum. 'Lena, I'm glad that you've got religious fever, but please don't try and convert me.' He pointed to himself. 'I've seen this thing before. When someone's got problems, instead of looking within themselves for the answer they look to 'God' to solve their problems. The thing that I can't understand though, is why? If God knows everyone and everything, why did he put the pressure on the person in the first place? To teach them a lesson? For punishment? To make them turn to him? Why? That doesn't speak to me about love. About caring. About goodness. Next, Lena, you'll be telling me that I have to have faith. Answer me this. Where do I buy it, because I haven't got any extra strength to conjure it up, or any extra money.' Dad stood up and walked across to the sink, dumping his plate, knife and fork into the bowl of soapy water.

When Dad got to the door he turned and said, 'Tell me when God showers down some money, enough to leave this dump and start afresh somewhere nice, okay.' He slammed the door.

My appetite disappeared in the momentary silence that filled the room after Dad had gone. The same must have happened to Niecy and Mum too, as they both laid down their knives and forks.

Niecy placed her hand on Mum's hand and told her, 'Mum, you have to go with what you believe. The strength of your convictions will be contested, criticised and challenged. But so what? If you believe in them strongly, nothing or no one can make you change your mind.'

Mum smiled. 'You're right, love. I know what I have in my heart is true. I can understand that people have been martyred for their faith and haven't renounced Christ.'

'That's a bit extreme, Mum,' laughed Niecy. It broke the sombre atmosphere.

'All your father's concerned about at the moment is building up his bank balance. Well, he'll be pleased to know that I'm doing a night shift on Christmas Day, which is paid at double time and the nursing home pay for my taxi home. The last time I worked on Christmas Day was before I was married. I don't want to do it, but I'm the newest member of staff. Everyone else has sorted out their days off, and I'm left with what everyone else doesn't want to do.' Mum sighed.

'Mum, that's awful. We've *always* spent Christmas together,' I said, dismayed.

Later that night, I sat in my room listening to a song by Trademark, a really cool R&B group. Beri had bought me their CD for Christmas after I told him I liked them. He said that he had some other stuff put aside for my birthday.

The music soothed me, and I drifted off into a daydream.

We were on a sun-kissed island. Beri and I were

smooching to soft music on a moonlit beach. I was wearing a long flowing dress. The breeze was cool and gentle. As we swayed to the music of the orchestra…

My mobile phone rang.

I snatched it up from the bedside table. I smiled, thinking it must be Beri.

'Hi Beri, I was just dreaming of you.'

'No, its not Beri, it's Tia. Hi, how are you?'

I swallowed my disappointment, and I felt a bit foolish too. 'I'm fine, how are you?'

'Great. Have you heard from Beri recently?'

I sat up. 'Why, is something wrong?'

'Are you busy tomorrow?'

'Yes, fairly.' I didn't want to go to another church meeting. Even though Tia has in no way been pressuring me to come to her church, I didn't want to get caught out and get another invitation.

'Oh.'

'Why do you ask, and why did you want to know if I had heard from Beri?'

She hesitated, than said quietly, 'I've just found out that he's been arrested.'

'*What?*' I shouted so loudly I must have deafened Tia. 'What do you mean, he's been arrested? You're joking.'

'I'm not.' Tia sounded deadly serious.

'Can you come round now?' I pleaded. I was frightened.

'It's late, Lois. Look, I'll see if I can find out more, and I'll call you tomorrow.'

'No, don't call, come round.'

12

Mum monopolised Tia as soon as she entered the flat the next day.

'Would you like a drink?' Mum had already put a glass and a carton of fruit juice on the kitchen table.

'Thanks,' smiled Tia.

I sat opposite her and watched how she talked so easily with Mum. Tia gave off such warmth that you couldn't help responding positively. But that warmth wasn't penetrating me. In fact, I felt quite cold. No, more than cold – frozen. I wanted Tia to myself. I wanted to know what had happened to Beri. I had tried calling his mobile last night, but I just kept getting his voicemail.

'How are you finding church, Mrs Darnell?' I marvelled at Tia's calmness as I furiously tried to give her the eye to cut the talk, and come up to my room. I wanted information – and now!

'Oh, I'm really enjoying myself.'

I looked from one to the other. 'Lois, I know what you're going to say, but I did tell you that I was going to the same church as Tia. You weren't listening.'

'I, eh, I…' That wasn't what was on my mind, but I managed to dreg up a watery smile to make them think I was following their conversation.

Mum and Tia laughed. 'Her head's been filled with Christmas and her birthday. She hasn't got room for anything else.' Mum smiled.

I knew that she was hinting at my preoccupation, but I let it run pass me.

I was just about to ask Tia to come to my room when Mum said, 'Tia, I was reading the Bible the other day, and something that Jesus said puzzled me.'

Would you believe it! I wanted to scream. I didn't want to sit here listening to some theological rubbish. I shot to my feet and told Tia, 'I'll be up in my room when you're finished.' I stormed out the room.

I knew it was bad manners, but since I had spoken to Tia on the phone, I'd been on edge. Surely she must know that? But no, she locks herself into a tête-à-tête with my Mum. I wouldn't mind so much, but she's supposed to be my friend!

I paced up and down in my room with my mobile phone in my hand, waiting for Tia to come upstairs and waiting for Beri to answer his mobile. The carpet would soon have a worn tract through the middle of it as I marched up and down. The suspense of not knowing what was going on was eating into me. My mind had been jam-packed with Beri, even more so since Tia called me last night. Normally my thoughts of him are happy ones, but not today.

What could have happened? Was he involved in a fight? Was he driving under the influence of alcohol? Had he killed someone? I shook my head at how ridiculous my thinking had become.

Beri.

Every day, I have Beri for breakfast, Beri for dinner and Beri for tea. He constantly phones me and I am able to see him most days (the other few days I'm at school). I'd still been keeping my eye out for letters from school or the education authorities about my frequent truanting. But somehow in my warped thinking, it seemed so right to be out and about with Beri that I didn't let it bother me.

My life has changed for the better since I started going out with him. I don't have to keep looking over my shoulder at school any more. Whenever I see the three horrors, they leave me alone.

Beri seems to live in his car. When I'm with him, we drive all over London. He has friends in Brixton (south), Tottenham (north) and Shepherd's Bush (west), and everywhere in between!

Money's no object to him. I decided that he must earn a load from his uncle's business. Whatever I want, I get. It reminds me of how I used to live in Hartsenwood. Having a meal in a restaurant and not looking at the prices is heady. If we go shopping, it's become so that I pick up some make-up or something for my hair, or a pair of shoes that I love – anything, and Beri picks up the tab. He never complains.

'You're making me become so decadent,' I told him once, smiling.

'Meaning…?' he wore a half-grin. That's another thing about him that I love– he isn't embarrassed to admit it when he doesn't know something. 'Meaning, my value system has plunged to an all-time low. You spoil me.'

That made him laugh. 'That's what guys do to beautiful, articulate girls.'

How could I not have such a depth of feeling for him that it was slowly consuming my life!

A tap on the door made me take one leap from the window to the door, tearing it open.

'About time too!' I snapped.

As Tia looked at me, her lips pursed up. 'Pardon?'

'Did you or did you not come to see me?' I was being horrible, but I didn't care.

'I came to your house, and your mum started to speak to me, was I supposed to ignore her and—'

'Yes!' I shouted. My hands were on my hips and I was ready for a fight. Couldn't Tia see that I was wound up? Any minute now I was going to explode.

'Bye.'

I must have blinked about twice in the time it took for Tia to spin around and fly back down the stairs.

I was mortified. She was the link to any information I could get about Beri.

'I'm sorry, I'm sorry!' I shouted at Tia's retreating back. She slowed down and turned to face me.

'I'm sorry, Tia, for shouting at you. If you wait a minute I'll just get my coat and we'll go for a walk, is that okay?' I asked cautiously. I didn't want to frighten her away.

'No, that's alright, I'll wait.'

In a flash, I grabbed my things.

The day was cold. Tia linked her arm through mine. I was glad that she wasn't upset with me. If it had been the other way round and she had shouted at me, we would not be walking down any road – that's for sure.

We walked in silence. I was itching to ask about Beri, but Tia didn't seem in too much in a hurry to tell me.

'Shall we go and sit in the Grassroots café and have a hot chocolate?' she suggested. I was ready to agree with anything she said.

'Yeah, that's great.'

The blast of heat and the low murmur of voices met

us as soon as the door of Grassroots was open. It was a West Indian café many local people used. Not just black people, but those of different nationalities, seemed to blend in with the colourful décor.

We found a corner table and slid in. It was a bit of a tight squeeze. Tia got the drinks and two slices of carrot cake. I'd lost my appetite, but the smell of the cake cut into my senses. I nibbled at the edges. Half the cake disappeared.

'Right,' said Tia.

I put my plate down. A knot formed in my stomach.

'Yeah, go on.' I was eager to find out what had happened to Beri.

'First of all, I wasn't wilfully holding back any information about Beri. I was ready to tell you as soon as I came to your place. But I couldn't be rude to your mum, could I, and then when you shouted at me, I wasn't having it.'

Tia was like a nagging toothache. I kept my mouth shut.

She looked at me over the rim of her cup. 'Okay, from what I've heard, two girls were shoplifting up the West End. How they could have thought that they would get away with it with all those cameras about I don't—'

'What has that to do with Beri?' I interrupted.

Tia held up her hand in my face. 'Will you listen?'

I shut up.

'The store detective followed them. The trail lead them to Beri waiting in a van, packed sky high with stolen goods.'

'Never!' I slammed my hand down on the table. 'Beri isn't like that.'

Tia took a sip from her cup. She shrugged her shoulders. 'Okay, if that's what you think.'

'Beri's not a thief.' I pointed my finger in her face. I was angry with her for telling me such rubbish.

'He must have been just a passenger in the van. I don't believe he was behind it, as you've tried to imply.'

'You could be right.'

'See,' I said triumphantly, folding my arms.

Tia looked at me. I was willing her to challenge me, but she changed tactics.

'What has Beri told you about himself?'

I avoided Tia's question. 'What police station is he in?'

'One in the West End. Come on, tell me what he has said about himself, and about me.'

'About you, that you could have had a thing going between you but you got all religious. And about himself, that he's at college, and he works for his uncle.'

Leaning back in her chair, Tia said, 'Have you ever wondered why he doesn't go to college that often, then?'

'He does. When I'm at school, he goes to college. Anyway, he has to do a lot of his work at home.'

'He hasn't changed.'

'What do you mean?'

'He has everything sussed out. The thing is, though, one day, it will all come on top.'

'Meaning what?'

'The bottom will drop out of his world, and anyone else who is attached to him will fall down with him.'

'Are you warning me, Tia?'

'How are you hearing me, Lois?'

'It's as though you're warning me.'

'If that's how you're seeing it, so be it.'

'There's no need for any warning. Beri is cool and together. He's not a criminal. Some of his friends might be, but not him.'

When Beri and I were out and about meeting different people, I thought that some of them looked and acted very suspiciously. But it was none of my business. Nor Tia's. I believed Beri when he'd said he felt that Tia still fancied him. Maybe that was true. I noted how quick she was to come and give me bad news about him.

Finishing her drink, Tia stood up. 'Do you fancy going down the market, Lois?'

'Not really.'

Tia put her hands on the table and leaned towards me. 'There's no point fretting about Beri. If he hasn't done anything wrong, he'll be alright. I'm sure he can look after himself.'

That was true, I thought – he definitely could look after himself.

'Come on then, let's go.'

The market was packed. Being a very cold day, I assumed that most people would still be at home or have gone shopping at an indoor mall. In Marshton Hills they obviously did things differently.

'I wish I'd brought some money with me, those trousers look really nice.' I held a pair of flared black trousers against myself.

'Seven ninety-nine, love,' said the stallholder.

'Will you have any next week?'

'Don't know love, they're selling like hot cakes.'

'If Beri were here he would have bought them for

me,' I said wistfully.

Tia rolled her eyes. We walked around the market looking at all the things we liked, but couldn't afford. Tia was good company. She told me a bit about her friends.

'Hi, Tia.'

We both looked round. I recoiled in fright. It was Carmel with a woman who I thought must be her mother.

'Hi Linda, Carmel.'

I had been holding Tia's arm. She stiffened and I clutched it tighter.

'How's your mum, Tia?' asked Linda.

'Fine.' Tia wasn't getting herself into a cosy chat with them.

'How are you, Lois? Did you know that Beri's got himself into a spot of trouble? But he's alright now,' grinned Carmel.

'Yeah, I know.' I was shaking, but I must have hidden it well, as Carmel hadn't picked up on it.

The grin was wiped off her face. 'He phoned you already?'

'See you, Tia. Bye.' Linda looked at me and pushed Carmel. I half-turned in time to see Carmel's mum giving her a dig in the arm.

I whipped out my phone.

'The battery's down. I should have charged it overnight. Beri's probably been trying to call me, but he's not been able to get through.'

'Probably. Do you want to go home now?'

'Yeah, I do. I've got to get my phone charged up.'

I left Tia on the bus after I got off at my stop. I ran home. As I came through the shop, Dad said, 'A couple of people were looking for you. Who are they, school friends?'

'A couple of people. Who?'

A customer came in. Dad smiled at her and casually walked towards her. 'Can I help you?'

I went upstairs. I knew there was no point questioning Dad further when he had a customer.

Mum was stirring a big pot of chicken soup when I went into the kitchen.

'Do you know who came to see me, Mum?'

She shrugged. 'I didn't see them, but your dad said it was Chloe and Tony, I think.'

'Oh, alright.'

In my room I fretted. Who on earth were Chloe and Tony?

13

'Oh, Beri, I can't accept this.' The smooth fabric of the Versace blouse was like water flowing through my hands.

'Sure you can, babes, nothing's too good for you.'

My mouth was fixed into a permanent grin. Since getting into Beri's car, he had given me my birthday presents one by one. I couldn't wait for my birthday to come. I just had to open them now.

I was so happy that Beri and I were still going out with each other. I thought back to not so long ago when he had been falsely arrested. It was a terrible time.

When I saw him later that evening, I threw my arms around him and clung onto him like moss on a rock.

'Oh, Beri, I was so frightened.'

He hugged me tight. 'No need, Lois.' His mouth close to my ear, he whispered, 'It was all a mistake.'

'That's what I told Tia. She was so quick to paint a bad picture of you.'

He laughed. 'The girl still has it bad for me.'

I wasn't sure about that, but I let it go.

'Do you know some guy called Tony, and a girl called Chloe? Only they came to the shop to see me. I've never heard of them.'

He took a step back and creased up into laughter. 'Oh man, that was funny. When I got into your shop, your dad pounced on me. He thought I was a potential customer. He asked me what I was looking for, what kind of a budget I had, what size feet I had. Lois,' Beri had tears in his eyes he was laughing so much, 'your Dad is one *efficient* guy.' He wiped his eyes.

I didn't like the way this was going. The thing is, my dad is my dad. Having someone taking the mickey out of him was unpleasant. Much as I like Beri, he really had no right to do it. But I couldn't bring myself to tell him.

'Tony, man, Tony. Tony's the name. That's what I told your dad *after* he must've talked about ten minutes straight,' he waved his hand in the air, 'about buying a pair of his trainers.'

He smiled at me. I couldn't smile back. Beri seemed oblivious.

Quietly I said, 'Why didn't you tell him your real name, and who was the girl?' That was what I *really* wanted to know.

'Tony is my middle name, and I sometimes use that. The girl is my cousin, Chloe James.'

He looked into my eyes, and stroked my face. 'That ole green-eyed monster is not rearing its ugly ole head?' He kissed my lips.

'No.'

'Good.'

* * *

Christmas Day was the first Christmas in which the presents under our tree had been sparse, and the first in which we, as a family, hadn't spent the whole twenty-four hours together. Mum had left for work at 8 pm, and Dad had planted himself in front of the TV with a bottle of whiskey and a glass.

Mum had gone to church in the morning. She had

wanted me to come, but I couldn't be bothered to get out of bed. It's funny you know, Mum has really changed. It hasn't been an overnight thing, but she now seems to radiate a warmth that she didn't have before. I have to admit too, that Mum used to be a bit of a show-off, especially when we lived in Hartenswood. Whenever family or friends came to visit us, Mum would take them around the house, and display her new curtains, or whatever it was that she had recently brought. Dad and I used to laugh about it – 'It's just the way Mum is.'

But not now. Besides the fact that there's nothing in the flat that would impress anyone, it seems that Mum just isn't interested in those sorts of things anymore.

Just like Tia.

Niecy was out with friends, which had really upset Dad, but there was nothing he could do. And then there was me. It seemed as though, once again, I was invisible. Beri had called me on my mobile to wish me a merry Christmas, and when I told him that it wasn't very merry, and that I was spending the evening in my bedroom, he told me he would pick me up after Mum had gone to work.

Beri parked the car under a lamppost, its dim light casting shadows all around us. The engine was running to keep the heat on. It was quite cosy.

I had put some of the presents across the dashboard, and I had a few on my lap. It was like Aladdin's cave. Beri had bought mostly clothes for me. I didn't know how I was going to hide them from Mum, but I would make up a lie about where I got them when the time came. I didn't think that Mum would notice, to be truthful, but I wasn't going to take any chances.

Beri placed his hand at the back of my neck. His dreamy eyes searched my face.

'You're beautiful, you know. You and I could really be something together. Something special.'

My toes tingled, and I giggled out of embarrassment. He leaned across to me and lightly kissed my lips. Every nerve ending in my body was charged up.

Tenderly, he stroked my face. I couldn't be sure, but I thought I saw tears in his eyes. This guy is so emotional, I thought.

'Lois, I keep asking myself – why am I so attracted to you? Why? Your looks are fine, but it's something beyond that. But what is it? And you know, it has just come to me. My mum. You look like her when she was about your age. The pictures that I have seen of Mum could easily have been you. It's incredible.'

'Really, Beri, that's unbelievable,' I whispered.

'It's true.' He nodded. 'I've told her all about you, and she would like to meet you when she's back in London.'

Beri had told me that his Mum wasn't fully recovered from her illness, and had decided to spend Christmas in Bristol with her sister. He had spent the day with his older brother and his family.

The car had become quite hot. Taking my jacket off, I laid it on the back seat. Beri's eyes were all over me and I felt self-conscious. Slowly, he pulled me towards him, and held me tight.

'I think I'm falling in love with you, Lois. I can't seem to stop myself.'

His words sounded a bit corny, but at the same time

they touched a need in me for someone to say nice things to me. And for me to feel good about myself. I rested my head against his chest. He smelt nice and fresh. Sighing, I thought of all the pain that I had endured recently, and how being loved and cuddled by Beri just seemed so right.

A car pulled up alongside us. It cruised past then stopped. I barely registered it as my mind was so engrossed with Beri and the moment.

Thump!

A dark figure loomed at my window, followed by more thumping. I jumped, hitting my head against Beri's chin.

'Who's that?' My first thought was that it must be Dad. Then we heard a familiar voice yelling, 'Get out that car right now!'

Carmel.

She was tugging the door handle. I thanked God that I had locked it when I had got in.

Her eyes were blazing, her hair was sticking out at all angles, and she was raving mad.

Thump. Thump. Thump.

It seemed as though she was trying to break her way into the car.

'I've had enough now, Beri, get away from her!' she screamed.

Clutching Beri's arm I whispered in fright, 'What does she mean?'

'Beri, tell her now, tell her right NOW!' Carmel started to kick the car.

Pursing his lips Beri growled, 'Wait here.'

He didn't have to convince me. Carmel was in one foul mood.

He seemed to get to her side in one swoop. She was pointing her finger in his face and started to give him a mouthful of abuse. Beri grabbed her none-too-gently by the arm. Pain contorted her face as he dragged her screaming and kicking up the road. He took her up to the corner. It was a bit difficult to see what was happening – the window was steamed up. I hoped he was giving her a taste of her own medicine. My palms were sweaty and I was shaking. I felt tempted to slip out of the car and go home. But I couldn't. I wanted to know what had provoked Carmel. And how did she know we were here?

The car windows had misted up even more now that the engine was off. Wiping the clouded-up window, I screwed up my eyes, trying to see Beri and Carmel. They were still at the corner, but it seemed that Carmel had calmed down. Beri had his arm around Carmel's waist, and their faces were very, very close.

Were they kissing?

Goose pimples sprang up all over my skin, like salt grains on an egg. I rubbed the window frantically, but I couldn't see properly. Carmel was resting her head on Beri's shoulder. Maybe he was consoling her. But why were they so close? I wanted to open the door and call to him, but I didn't want to risk Carmel responding. My stomach flipped over and over and over. Why was he taking so long to talk to her, and it seemed so... *intimate*? Was he kissing her or was that my imagination? Just when I thought that I would burst with impatience, Beri walked Carmel back to the parked car and helped her to get in. The car drove away – with Carmel inside. I thought I would feel better, but I didn't.

Beri slipped into the driver's seat and started the engine. I sensed that his mood had changed. He seemed different. What could Carmel have said to make him change towards me?

My mouth was dry. 'What was the problem?' I said sharply. I was trying to compose myself, and appear cool, calm and collected, but it was hard.

Calmly, Beri turned to me. 'Nothing much.'

I was livid. 'Nothing much? Are you kidding? That girl's crazy. She would have smashed your car to bits, and us with it, the way she was carrying on!' I shouted. I was really upset that he had spent time trying to placate her when it was me he should have been comforting.

He smiled. 'You're jealous, babes.'

'What?' I screeched. 'Jealous of *her*? You're mad. Carmel hates me, and it's *she* who can't stand the fact that *we* are together. It should be *her* you're talking to about jealousy.'

There was some truth in his words. I wanted to really ask him if he had been kissing her, but somehow I just couldn't say it.

'Listen, Babes. Carmel's dad wants to get back with her mum, who doesn't want him, right. Just before Christmas, he turned up out of the blue. Her mum wanted him out of the house, they had a row. He's turned up tonight, slapped Carmel and her mum around and…'

'But how did she know to come here?'

'I told her I was coming to see you, and if she needed any help, this is where I'd be,' he said calmly, as though I was asking him for the time.

'*You* told *her* that you'd be with *me*?'

'Yeah. What's your problem?'

My mouth opened, but no words came out. I was shocked.

'Listen, Lois. You and I are going to go places okay, but you don't own me – get it? I have to look out for Carmel, she's special to me too. You got that?'

'But Beri, you said that we…'

Beri made a big show of looking at the clock on the dashboard. 'It's getting late, Lois. I have to love you and leave you.' Clipping his seatbelt, his lips broke into a smile that didn't reach his eyes. I shivered.

'What's wrong, Beri? Did Carmel say something about me?'

Shaking his head he said, 'No. Look, I have to run now. Business. I'll call you soon.'

He was dismissing me. I was really hurt at his attitude, but I couldn't show it. He even helped me to gather up my presents. He was making it clear to me that he wanted me out of his car. Clutching my presents under my arm, I clambered out of his car. Just as I went to shut the door, he called me. I stuck my head back into the car. For a moment we looked at each other, then he said, 'Hold on.'

He got out of his car and walked round to me. He gently held me in his arms. 'Listen, I'm not getting rid of you, it's just that I've got to see my mum.' He kissed the top of my head.

The tears that had built up were dampened down at his words. 'It's okay,' I sniffed. I tried to smile as I said, 'It's Christmas Day, anyway, so I can't blame you for wanting to spend time with her.'

I didn't feel much better as he gave me a last peck

on the lips. He got back into his car and drove off.

He says he's going to see his mum, but what if he's really meeting up with Carmel?

Tiptoeing into the flat, I crept past the front room. The door was ajar. Peeking inside, I could see Dad's head lolling to one side. The television was on, but Dad was out for the count. Good.

Up in my room, I pored over the gifts that Beri had given me. The perfume was divine, and the blouse and dress that he had got me were really nice. How he knew what size to get for me I don't know. I suppose that being a bit 'arty' must make him more aware than other guys of the different sizes in girls. I must admit that I was overwhelmed. He had given me more than anyone else this year. He was so thoughtful. When I opened the perfume box, out dropped a little note saying: I love you!

He is soooo nice.

Whilst showering I thought about what had happened tonight. The only sensible conclusion that I could come to was that Beri was just being his wonderful self in trying to dry up Carmel's tears by holding her close to him. It must have worked, as there had not been any sign of madness from her afterwards.

Lying in bed, I couldn't sleep. Beri was so much in my mind it was hard to relax and let sleep take over. I replayed everything that happened that night and I felt so loved and wanted by him, but there was something that kept bugging me.

Were Beri and Carmel dating? Is that why she was so angry with me, and with him?

Where was he now – with Carmel?

A cat was miaowing to his friend. The cat

conversation cut into my thoughts, and I rolled onto my side.

Another thought hit me. Beri had first told me that his mum was with her sister in Bristol. But then he had said that he was going home to spend the rest of the evening with her. How could he when she was miles away?

My mind was racing. I switched on the bedside lamp and keyed Beri's mobile number.

No answer.

I scrolled through my address book and called him again.

No answer.

By the third time my pulse was beating at double its normal pace. Why won't he answer his phone? I thought to myself. Beri hadn't given me his home number otherwise I would have called him there.

I decided to ring him once more and if he didn't answer, I would leave it.

It rang three times. I was just about to disconnect when a voice said, 'Hello?'

It was a girl's voice.

'Hello,' I replied. 'I think I have the wrong number.' I thought that in my impatience to contact Beri, I must have punched in a wrong digit.

What she said next jolted me. 'I don't think so. Is it Beri you wanted, Lois?'

Maniacal laughter assaulted my eardrums. I was too shocked to answer.

It was Carmel.

Not waiting for me to say something, she went on, 'Well, Lois, I'm sorry to have to tell you this, but—'

The line went dead.

14

Frantically, I redialled again and again.

Nothing.

The phone had been switched off.

I tried to sleep, but it was impossible. I tossed and turned. I got up and restlessly stalked my room, backwards and forwards. My mind churned and over and I envisaged one hundred and one different scenarios as to what was happening between Beri and Carmel.

Could I have dialled the wrong number and it was Carmel's and not Beri's? Were their numbers so close that they differed by one digit? If Carmel was at Beri's house, or vice versa, why?

3.15 am.

I sat on the edge of my bed. Acid bore a burning track through my gut. My palms were clamming, and I was hot and cold alternately. I turned on my bedside lamp and picked up my mobile phone.

I punched in Beri's number. No answer.

I did it again, changing one digit. It rang. A croaky voice answered. 'Yes, who is it?'

It wasn't Beri, so I pressed the off button.

I went through about ten numbers, changing one digit each time. With each number my stomach would lurch, and bile would rise up in my gut. I was shaking so violently that the phone fell from my hands. Clasping my hands together I tried to still them. Finally I gripped them with my knees. The night was thick darkness around me, the weak light through the window couldn't dispel it.

The thought that Beri and Carmel could be an item revolved around my mind endlessly.

Is that why she was screaming and kicking the car?

Were they really kissing at the end of the street and it wasn't just my imagination?

What about Beri and me?

I couldn't sit still. I began pacing up and down. This was worse than when I had heard he had been arrested.

What should I do? What should I do?

I wished I knew where Beri lived. I would go there right now and confront him. I had a rough idea where Carmel lived but, for obvious reasons, there was no way I would go there.

The cold was beginning to bite my hands and feet. Reluctantly, I climbed back into bed. I sat up and wrapped the duvet around me.

Rocking to and fro, I tried to get Beri's handsome face out of my mind. The more I tried to erase it, the more it seemed to focus clearly. Tears slowly fell down my cheeks as the shape of Beri's face, his eyes, his nose, his lips imprinted themselves explicitly in my mind's eye.

The slow tears quickened pace and soon a torrent overtook me.

The times we kissed seemed almost real again, and I could feel the heat of his face close to mine.

I buried my head in the duvet, trying to shut all the images out. It didn't work. When the word *love* bombed unannounced into my head, I wasn't able to resist it.

I lay on my side and the tears continued to fall.

Beri had indicated so sweetly, so clearly, that he was falling in love with me.

He had made it seem that it was something that he had no control over.

But even more than that, I knew that I loved him.

Where did that leave me?

* * *

'Eat up, Lois, I cooked this meal especially for you as I know you love jerk chicken and rice. What about that Caesar salad, you love that, too.'

Mum eyed me with suspicion. I wanted to see Beri over the New Year. But it didn't happen. It had been ten days since I had last seen Beri, and I had hardly eaten a thing. How I was going to cope with the first day back at school tomorrow was anyone's guess – but that was the last thing on my mind. My clothes were hanging off me and I had dark circles under my eyes. My stomach was constantly churning. I could just about keep water down. Beri had phoned me twice in ten days, and each time it was a hurried conversation about how much he loved me and would see me soon. I tried to get a few words in, but he quickly talked over them.

'Lois? Lois?' Mum's face was full of concern. 'I've been talking to you and you've been in a world of your own. What's wrong?'

I kept my eyes on my plate. I had managed to keep out of Mum's way for days. It hadn't been too difficult, especially as she works shifts, but that still hadn't put her off hassling me when she could.

Dad got up from the table, burped then said, 'If I didn't know any better, I'd think that Lois is lovesick.'

I was shocked that Dad had hit the nail on the head. Without waiting to be interrogated by Mum, I made my exit.

Up in my room I drew the curtains as the daylight hurt my eyes. In bed, I wrapped up in the duvet and tortured myself about the last time I had seen Beri, and the phone conversation with Carmel.

Having got no clear answers about the whole situation, I couldn't bring it to resolution. Every question I had had drawn a blank so far.

A knock at my door made me huddle under the duvet.

The door opened.

'Lois, are you sleeping?'

I didn't respond to Mum. Maybe she would think that I was sleeping and leave me alone. No such luck.

'I didn't think you could be asleep so quickly, you've only been up here for twenty minutes. Come on, sit up, I want to talk to you.'

I groaned quietly as Mum pulled back the curtains and plonked herself on my bed.

Mum began stroking my hair. I wanted to cry, but I dug my fingernails into my upper arm and bit my lower lip. I needed to be in control of myself to deal with Mum.

'Right, Lois. I want you to know that starting from next month, I will be doing a refresher course in nursing. I can't tell you how glad I am. Working at the old folks' home is so stressful. When the nurse manager refused to let me have Christmas Day and New Year's Day off, I thought that that was the last straw. I prayed that God would direct me and help me and he did. I felt that the right thing to do would be to start my nursing again and go for it. I've been accepted on a course in February. Isn't that marvellous? Lois, Lois, are you listening?' Mum tugged the duvet. I held on tighter.

'Yes, Mum.' I was happy she was talking about herself – that meant she would leave me alone.

'It also means that I will have more time at home with you. What do you think about that?'

'Great,' I mumbled.

Mum didn't speak for a moment. 'Lois, something is wrong, isn't it? Tell me what it is, maybe I can help?'

The miserable, wretched feelings that were swirling around me hit a nerve and I began to sob. For days I had been secretly trying to cope with the emotional pain that I was experiencing, but I couldn't keep it inside any longer.

Mum leaned over me and drew me to her. My head was buried in Mum's ample chest, and she rocked me. I could hear Mum cooing above the agony of tears that cascaded from me.

'Okay, my darling.' Mum's voice was like a soothing balm that helped to stem the flood of tears that seemed to have no end.

For a while we just clung to each other as the tears faded away. Silence crept into the room, and for a while everything was still. My fuddled mind began to shift and move as Beri's face once again loomed to the forefront of my mind.

Mum was sure to ask me what was wrong. What was I going to tell her? Taking a few deep breaths I thought it would be better if I launched in with a light-on-detail version of Beri and I.

'Mum, I…' My voice croaked as I tried to get the

words out.

Mum pulled me away from her and looked down at me. I didn't look up at her as I knew her penetrative eyes would know something was missing from what I had to say.

'I met this guy.'

'Hmmm.'

'And he, eh, he's really nice, and I like him a lot.'

'But why are you crying? And Lois, these tears are deep and troubled.'

I wished Mum would let me finish. 'Yes, yes, I know, Mum. The thing is,' I took another breath and licked my lips. 'The thing is, I really, really like him and he really likes me.'

'Is it a boy you've met at school?'

'Yeah,' I lied. I didn't want to go into the Carmel and school situation. Well, not yet anyway. I just couldn't bring myself to talk about it with anyone except Tia.

'So, why are you crying, then? You're not pregnant, are you?' said Mum worriedly.

'No way!' I shouted.

'Well, what is it, then?'

'It's because, because…'

Mum sighed. 'Can't you think of a lie quick enough? Now come on, Lois, tell me the truth so that I can work out how to help you.'

My temper flared up a bit. 'Mum, how can you help me, eh? You're always out working. If it wasn't for you having these three days off in a row, you would be none the wiser about how I was feeling.'

'But Lois, I have to work now. You know that. You're a big girl now, and your dad and I feel that we can leave you alone, because you've proved to us that you're so grown up. Have we overestimated you?'

Swallowing quickly, I retorted, 'Of course I'm grown up, and anyway, I can sort out my life for myself, okay?'

'Now listen, Lois, there's no need to take that tone of voice with me. You are clearly upset and badly so. As your mother, I want to know what's going on. And now.'

I tore myself out of her arms and flopped back against my pillows, turning my face away from Mum. What was the point? Mum never gave me the chance to finish what I wanted to say.

'I'm waiting.'

I wondered how I should start. Once again, the thought entered my head as to whether or not I should tell my mum about Carmel. I had thought of this moment when I could pour out all my fears and worries and let Mum take over. But I knew her reaction would make the situation worse, not better. How could I tell her about Beri? That I had fallen in love with him? That he had another girl, I think? That he was older than me and he had money and owned his own car?

She would flip.

Mum coughed.

'Alright. I met this guy and I have a lot of feelings for him. I've never felt this way before about anyone. My mind is totally consumed with thoughts of him. And I know that he loves me.'

Mum's lip was twitching. She was restraining herself from commenting.

'I love him, Mum.' We looked at each other for a

brief second.

'Are you sure it's love and not infatuation or maybe even obsession?' Mum's tone was flat. I could see that she was trying very hard to restrain herself from saying too much. I wondered how long that would last. 'This is your first boyfriend, Lois. How old is he? What are his parents like? You haven't told me much about him. And besides all that, what is his name?'

I sat up. 'Mum, you've just asked me about ten quick-fire questions. How can we have any kind of conversation if it's purely on a question and answer basis?'

'I understand what you're saying, Lois, but you have to realise where I'm coming from. You look ill and you're going around in a deep depression. You haven't eaten a decent meal in days, and you're biting everyone's head off. Then you say you're in love?' Mum said incredulously.

An ear-splitting crash, followed by breaking glass, pierced the air. Mum and I shuddered at the impact. We were obviously getting used to our noisy surroundings as we both ignored it and continued our chat.

'Lois, I just want to try and understand—'

'Mum, I've told you everything. What more could you possibly want to know?'

Mum pleaded with me. 'Lois, I'm worried about you. Look at yourself in the mirror and—'

Heavy footsteps thudded up the stairs. The bedroom door flew open and Dad shouted, 'Come down, Lena, the shop window's been smashed!'

Mum shot out the door and I was behind her like her shadow.

On entering the shop, we both gasped in shock and horror at the carnage. The shop's main big glass window was shattered. Shards of glass lay haphazardly on the floor. A gaping, jagged hole was all that remained of the window.

'Oh Lord,' exclaimed Mum. 'Who could have done this, and why?' She held her cheeks in her hands and her mouth was wide open.

'I'll kill them, I'll strangle them with my bare hands,' ranted Dad through clenched teeth. He stomped around the shop, glass crunching beneath his feet.

'Why, why, why?' Dad eyes wildly roved around from the window to the broken glass on the floor. He stormed over to the counter, and bashed his fist on it repeatedly.

'These people are jealous that I've only just come here and I'm already making money. Don't they know how hard I'm working to make a success of this business? Evil, that's what they are, evil.'

'Ron, you don't know who has done this. How can you say that it is these people? What people are you referring too?'

A brick with a piece of paper and an elastic band around the middle was lying not far from the back wall.

'Look, Mum,' I pointed to the brick. 'That brick might have been the cause of the smashed window.'

Mum tiptoed carefully over the glass-splintered floor and retrieved the brick. She removed the elastic band and opened the paper.

'Lena!' shouted Dad, 'Why did you pick that up, it'll have the evil criminal's fingerprints all over it!'

Screwing up her face, Mum read, 'Keep away from B.' She dropped the brick, the paper and the elastic band.

'Let me see.' Dad snatched it off the floor. His head was bent as he read the note. 'Right, I'm calling the police. This is more than vandalism, this seems like some sort of vendetta.' He walked round the other side of the counter, picked up the handset and began to punch the numbers in.

'Police, please.'

I was shocked. I felt rooted to the spot. It was crystal clear to me what the message was – KEEP AWAY FROM BERI. It must be Carmel, or someone she was able to persuade to do this.

The enormity of the broken window and the reason for it made fear overshadow me like a physical mass that filled every nerve and every cell in my body.

I fainted.

15

My French class was a blur. It was the first class after lunch, and my concentration was shot to pieces. My mind was stuck in a groove. I played the scene over and over.

Mum reviving me in the shop.

The police questioning us. 'Any known enemies? Do you owe money? Do you know who could have done such a thing? Did you see anyone?' The list was endless. No was the answer to every question.

The brick being bagged up and taken away, for evidence in court (but only if the perpetrators are caught?).

The glaziers who came and fitted the new window.

By the time we were left alone, I was exhausted. Mum and I were upstairs in the living room and Dad was in the shop. I think he thought if he kept vigil there, nothing more could happen.

'How are you feeling now, Lois?'

'Fine, Mum.' I felt dreadful, but I wasn't about to say so.

'Sure?' Mum's eyes stayed fixed on me. I was sitting in the armchair nearest to the television. I slipped my hands under my legs. I was shaking so much that I knew Mum would notice it.

'Lois.' Mum came and sat on the settee. She flicked the television off with the remote. Looking directly at me she said, 'Lois. Something is really bothering you. What is it?'

'Nothing, Mum, honest.' I looked towards her quickly and then I leaned back in the armchair. I wanted Mum to think that I had it all together.

She wasn't easily fooled.

Mum sat looking at me, which was worse than her talking. I could feel her eyes imploring me to turn and look at her. To say something, anything. I sat still, focusing my eyes on the pale sky through the window. I wondered what it would be like to be a carefree bird soaring aimlessly through the air. No worries. No problems.

Mum gently took my hand in hers. She began stroking my fingers.

'You're still my baby, Lois, and I love you.'

I wanted to pour out my troubles to Mum there and then. I was surprised, too, that Mum, who would usually be interrogating me, seemed content to just say a few words. I could see how much she was changing. The peace she'd said she felt inside since becoming a 'real' Christian was helping her to act and respond differently. She reminded me so much of Tia, and how she acts under difficult circumstances.

But here I was, a girl with a ton of unsolvable, painful problems that no one, anywhere, could resolve.

* * *

The bell ringing jolted me back to real life. School. I gathered up my books and slowly walked to the door. My last class was Information Technology. Hoisting my rucksack onto my back, I allowed myself a morbid grin when I thought how heavy it was, but that the problems in my head outweighed it a hundred times over.

'Lois.' I glanced around.

Jennifer and Neera.

My heart rate shot up a few notches. 'Yeah?' I tried to smile, but my lips were dry and stuck to my teeth.

'Nice Christmas?' grinned Neera.

'Did you have a smashing time?' laughed Jennifer. They both creased up with huge guffaws that had them rolling along the corridor.

Sweat bubbles broke out on my forehead and under my arms. My knees were about to collapse.

I couldn't talk as a large lump was blocking my throat. Taking deep breaths instead, I tried to steady myself. I really wanted to curl up and die. If only the floor would develop a gaping hole and swallow me.

I knew I had to keep walking. How I managed to put one foot in front of the other was a mystery, even to myself.

'Did you get some nice new clothes for Christmas, too?' said Neera coyly.

'I bet you got a Versace blouse and a lovely bottle of that perfume, eh, what's it called Neera, something beginning with D.' Jennifer snapped her fingers.

'Death!' squealed Neera in obvious delight at my discomfort. I kept walking, my eyes on the ground. It was hard to shut out their voices.

'Dirty,' Jennifer said with clenched teeth.

'Destroy,' growled Neera.

I tried to ignore them, but they were facing me, walking backwards. I was gritting my teeth trying to hold back the flow of tears, and to keep fear from showing on my face.

My mind was revolving and twirling. Suddenly, they stopped walking.

So did I.

Our eyes locked. Jennifer straightened herself up, towering over me. 'So. Altogether you had a sweet Christmas, and a wonderful birthday. Nice. With lots and lots of pressies. And you didn't have to do a thing for them. Yet.'

They gave me one long stare, and then they turned and walked off.

I didn't realise that I had been holding my breath, but as I groped the wall to steady myself, I exhaled deeply. A loud roar filled my ears, and the floor seemed to rise up to my face. How did they know? My mind refused to accept that Beri had told them. But how else could they know?

A chant of 'I'm not going to faint, I'm not going to faint, I'm not going to faint' repetitively echoed in my head. I stood up straight. My rucksack had slid to the floor. I bent down and picked it up. What to do?

A fraction of a second later I was making my way out of school. I wouldn't go to Information Technology. At the door, I heard someone calling my name. Having been caught out before, I decided not to listen to the voice.

'Lois, Lois, wait!'

It didn't sound like Jennifer, Neera or Carmel, so I stopped. It was Mrs Crofton.

Breathing heavily she said, 'You sure walk fast, young lady. Where are you off to?'

I tried to smile for her, but there was nothing inside of me that could bring a smile to my lips. I just stared at her.

She peered at me through her glasses. 'Are you okay?'

My bottom lip trembled and it wouldn't have taken much to break down and bawl my eyes out. But I didn't.

I clutched my mouth as a good excuse popped into my head. 'I've got toothache, and I've had to book an emergency dental appointment.'

Mrs Crofton looked at me disbelievingly. But she couldn't tell me that I hadn't got toothache – how would she know?

'Lois...' She was going to say something, but she was hesitant. She smiled again and shook her head. 'Have you informed your head of year?'

'I was just going to tell Ms Levine.'

'Don't worry, I'll let her know.' She looked at me again. She was waiting for me to volunteer some information. She would have a long wait. Instead, she walked with me to the door.

'How are you getting on?'

'Fine,' I mumbled. I needed to get out of the door before I ended up confessing everything. Then where would that leave me?

Mrs Crofton said something that completely threw me and made me wonder what she knew. 'How do you get on with Jennifer and Neera? They're very good friends with Carmel Lentiss, aren't they?'

We stood looking at each other for a fleeting second.

I didn't, or more correctly couldn't, answer her.

'They're tough girls.' She took a few steps back and said, 'Remember, you can come and speak to me any time, alright.' She was gone.

I hurried across the school grounds and through the gates. It wasn't that I had somewhere special to go, but what Mrs Crofton had said had shaken me up.

At the corner of the school road, I eased my rucksack off my back. The day had been going so well for me. Jennifer and Neera hadn't been in any of my classes until after lunch. I rubbed my head. Taking my mobile out of my pocket, I called Beri. I wanted an explanation of why he had told those girls about what he had bought me for Christmas.

What else could he have told them? Just before Christmas, he had asked me if I had ever slept with a boy before. He grinned when I said no. Our kisses were becoming so passionate, I wondered if it would lead us down that road. I was preparing myself for it – then, but not now. There was no guarantee that he wouldn't divulge our intimate secrets. And besides, my feelings towards him were changing.

I called him four times. Each time I got his voicemail. I called Tia – I needed to talk to someone. I got her voicemail too. She must be in a lesson with her phone switched off. I stood on the corner, not knowing what to do. When the first stream of pupils came through the gates, I called Tia again. This time she answered and said that she would meet me soon.

True to her word, Tia came running towards me a couple of minutes later. Was I glad to see her!

Tia has been such a good friend to me in the short time that I have known her. She seems to go out of her way for me. She isn't preoccupied with herself like Sophie or Lucy-Ann or any of my other friends in Hartenswood. She just gives herself freely. Was I pleased that we were friends!

We agreed that I would go to her house. I called

Dad and told him where I would be. I didn't want to go home.

All the way to Tia's house I told her about my run-in with Jennifer and Neera. Up in Tia's bedroom I went over and over the same scenario.

'Why, Tia? Why would Beri tell them about what he had bought me?' I was bewildered.

Tia offered me some sweets and sat on the floor opposite me, while I sat on her bed.

'Lois, you cannot conceive the type of person Beri is.' I was about to interrupt her, but she held up her hand. I said nothing.

'Listen to me. You've called me today because the truth is, you just won't accept that Beri has been mouthing off about your business to people. Remember when he got nicked for working with those shoplifters, right—'

'Yeah, but that's in the past now, and he said that he wasn't involved.'

Tia rolled her eyes. 'I don't believe him. Stealing is Beri's craft. No, no, no, let me finish.' She pointed to her chest. 'I've been there. I know the runnings.'

I stood up. 'This isn't helping me, Tia.' I was tearful. 'I just want to know why those girls knew everything. What has this got to do with Beri and you?' I pointed an accusing finger at her. 'You must still like him…'

'That's not true, Lois, and you know it!' Tia shot to her feet.

'Isn't it? Every chance you get you talk about Beri and how bad he is. You keep on about him because you still fancy him, and you can't bear the thought that he is with me. Carmel and her friends are the problem, not Beri. I'm looking for help here. Something which

I now realise you can't give.'

Tia's left hand was on her hip, and her right one was pointing at me. Through clenched lips, she said, 'You are a fool. When Beri reveals his true colours then you're really going to know all about it, believe me. He controls Carmel and her mates. And not only that, you want to check out with him what his relationship with Carmel *really* is. I'm surprised you don't know. But don't take my word for it, find out for yourself.'

My phone rang. I scrabbled through my pocket and pulled the phone out. Our eyes were locked on each other.

'Hello? Oh, hi Beri.' I gloated at Tia. 'I'm at Tia's house. Fine, fine. I'll see you then.'

Tia had turned away and pretended to busy herself in her wardrobe.

'Thanks for the chat.' My words were coated in sarcasm.

She looked at me and sighed. 'No problem. I hope it all works out for you.'

'It will.'

I grabbed my rucksack, and trotted down the stairs. My earlier moods of fear and then anger had dissolved with one phone call from Beri. I pushed aside any thought about why he had told Jennifer and Neera and whoever else about our relationship. I did want to know, but if I asked him, would I *really* want to hear his answer? If it was in my favour, yes. If not, I would rather not know.

I stood on the corner of Tia's road for half an hour.

Agitation was making me restless. I walked a little way up the road, and then turned and walked back again. I looked at my watch a million times. I called Beri so often that I felt like flinging my phone down and jumping on it. I got his voicemail every time.

Where was he?

Furtively, I glanced down Tia's road. The last thing I needed was for Tia to see me. This would prove her point that Beri was unreliable and everything else. Why was he keeping me standing waiting in full view for the world and his wife to feast their eyes on me?

In the time it took him to come, my eyes were trained to pick out his car from the hundreds that had already passed me and I spotted it way down the road. The car careered to a stop as I tried as hard as I could to walk towards it casually.

I halted when I saw a girl in the front seat. Her sandpaper complexion was made worse by thick make-up. Her eyebrows rose up to meet her purple and black hairline. Her lips were outlined with what looked like black shoe polish, and coloured with a shiny, glittering, pearly cream.

'What time do you call this?' I was angry more at seeing the girl than his being late.

He leaned across the girl and, winding down the window, smiled his gorgeous smile. 'Sorry, babes. I got held up. Jump in.'

With hand on hip I fumed, 'How can I, it's a two-door car.'

He nodded his head at the girl, who rolled up her eyes and slowly opened the door and climbed out. On her feet with the thickest, highest soles I have ever seen. I was expecting her to get in the back. Instead, she stood with one hand on the door and the other on her hip. Boredom was written across her face. She looked at her long silver and black painted talons.

'C'mon, girls, hurry up. Time is money.' Beri revved the engine. 'Get in the back, Lois.'

'What, but—'

The girl prodded me in the side. 'You heard what he said, get in.'

Flinging my rucksack on the back seat, I clambered in behind her. Beri drove off at great speed. The girl and Beri were chatting away. I was ignored. This was a new Beri. I had never seen him behave in this way before. Normally I had his undivided attention. He would shower me with presents and words that hit a place in my heart and sparked off loving messages to every part of my body.

Not so now.

What had happened to him?

The girl must have shared a hugely funny joke, as Beri threw back his head in wild abandoned laughter.

'What's the joke?' I asked.

'You wouldn't understand,' she replied. She took a cigarette out of her bag and lit it.

'They're bad for you, girl,' drawled Beri.

'Everything good is,' she laughed.

'Oh, babes, by the way,' Beri half-turned in his seat, 'this is my cousin, Chloe.'

'Oh, this is Chloe!' I exclaimed.

'Yeah, pleased to meet yer.' She didn't even bother to turn around.

I hadn't been taking much notice of where we were going. Beri drove the car up a ramp into a car park. He brought the car to a halt on the third floor. Both he and Chloe turned and faced me in the back seat.

Folding my arms, I wondered what was going on.

At first I thought Beri had some nice surprise for me. But I soon found out I was wrong.

'Lois, honey, I seem to have a bit of a problem.'

I didn't trust myself to speak. So I didn't.

'That Versace blouse I gave you at Christmas, or your birthday, I can't remember which. I need it back.'

'What? Are you mad? You gave that to me as a present. You can't take presents back.'

Chloe laughed and shook her head.

'Have you worn it yet?' he asked.

'No, but I've tried it on loads of times, so that's as good as wearing it. Anyway, why do you want it?'

He licked his lips. 'I need the money.'

I didn't let him continue. 'Sorry, you've completely lost me. What has needing money got to do with having the blouse back?'

'Is she slow or what, Beri?' Chloe hung over the seat so that she was right in my face. 'Watch my lips. The blouse can be taken back to the shop, and money can be returned. Okay? Got that?' She sat back in her seat, pursed her lips and folded her arms.

I looked from one to the other. There was something happening that I couldn't fathom.

The atmosphere in the car became eerie. I noticed a few car owners either getting in or out of their cars. I couldn't get out of Beri's car as I was penned in like a prisoner. Sweat began to trickle down my back. Something was really, really wrong. My breathing became more and more shallow.

'Look, Beri, I want to go home.'

'Soon,' he said. 'First, though, I need you to do a favour for me. Then you can keep the blouse and everything else I've given you.'

'No, no, it's okay. You can have the blouse back, it's better if you need the money that I just give it back to you.'

Beri grinned and looked at Chloe.

'She catches on fast. I told you she had brains.' He looked at me again. 'No, you're right. You can't take back presents that you've given. Forgive me, babes, I'm out of order. Listen up now. Chloe knows the score. All I want you to do is follow her. When she goes into a shop, follow her, but keep away from her. Got it?' He looked at me and I nodded. I didn't know what else to do.

'When you see that she's making her way to the door, I want you to create a disturbance. Scream, shout, fall to the floor, have a fit, anything, do what you have to. Just do something loud and distracting. Give Chloe a bit of time to get out the door, then you recover and come back to the car. But,' he pointed his finger at me, 'not straight away. Look around the mall for a short while. It's very important that you're not followed by security, right. Then come back to me.' He took my hand and squeezed it lightly.

'Got that?'

I shook my head. My bladder was full and I needed release. I whimpered, 'I can't do that, it's wrong.'

Beri squeezed my hand hard. My eyes popped wide with pain and my nose began to run.

'Wrong or right, you have to do it. Now get going.'

16

'Just keep a bit behind me. Don't get too close,' snarled Chloe.

I dropped back and waited for her to lengthen the distance between us. Hooking my fingers through my rucksack, I gripped the straps. I wished that I were million miles away from here. If only I had listened to Tia. She was right. The Beri that I had left in the car was not the same guy that I had been dating for these past few months. It must be his twin!

I had refused to get out of the car, thinking that he would take pity on me and say it was all a mistake and take me home. I couldn't have been more wrong.

He opened the car door and literally dragged me out. My initial reaction to his brutality was to punch him in the arm. He squeezed my upper arm so tightly that I couldn't catch my breath.

'You had better not mess this up,' Beri whispered. 'Carmel is just a phone call away.'

His eyes were like bullets. His breathing was shallow and his nostrils flared with each intake of breath.

It was the threat of Carmel that got me walking. Ahead of me, Chloe entered a store. I looked around me at the busy shoppers going about their business and I wanted someone to rescue me. It would be so easy to just walk off in the opposite direction and go home.

A mother and daughter were in front of me and as

they walked into the store that Chloe had entered, I slipped in behind them. At first, I couldn't see Chloe. Then I spotted her. She was over by the dress section. I made my way to the shoe section and asked the assistant if I could try on a pair of high-heeled sandals. I was so nervous that I couldn't do up the strap and the assistant had to do it for me. I stood up in the shoes and walked a couple of steps. I took them off and asked to try on another pair. I didn't know what else I should do, and it wasn't until I had taken off my sixth pair of shoes that I heard a commotion in the store.

'Get your hands off me!' screamed the voice of Chloe. The 'mother and daughter' that were in front of me when I first came in the store were on either side of Chloe. They must have been undercover store detectives. The security guard was close behind Chloe, talking into his walkie-talkie. My mouth gaped open. Everything seemed to happen so fast. A few more security guards came running into the store, and escorted Chloe to the back.

'Have you made your mind up? I think those cerise sandals with the flower in front suited you the best. And they're good value at twenty-four ninety-nine. Would you like to try them on again?'

My eyes were fixed on the door that Chloe had been taken through.

'Are you going to buy them?' The assistant's voice was frosty.

'I, eh, I'll try them on again.' I was stalling for time.

A couple of police officers soon walked into the store and headed for the door at the back. Other shoppers were trying hard not to gape at the retreating policemen. The assistant must have realised that I wasn't a serious shopper. I still had my school uniform on and my heavy rucksack was by my feet. The assistant was snatching up the shoes and putting them back into their boxes. Her actions were making me jumpy.

'Is that it then?' she hissed.

Numbly, I stood up. It was at that point that the door opened and a policeman came out, followed closely by Chloe and the other policeman. She was handcuffed. Her mouth was set in a hard line. She looked very angry.

'Alright, you don't have to pull so hard!' she shouted. Then Chloe began to resist the policemen. She tugged and fought and kicked. The policemen had a job trying to keep hold of her.

'What you staring at?' she screamed at a young girl as she passed by. The young girl jumped. By the time they got to the door, Chloe really went berserk. She was like a mad woman. The security guard held onto her shoulders and a policeman held each arm. They struggled to control her.

As the group crossed the store threshold, Chloe turned and looked quickly over her shoulder. Our eyes met. Hers burned with hatred. She spat on the ground. The policemen, who had obviously had enough of her by now, roughly grabbed her arms and frogmarched her away.

'You would've thought she would go quietly after getting caught,' said one woman.

'Nah, these young criminals think they have a right to nick what they like.'

'It's disgraceful. Hope she gets locked up for a long time.'

When I left the store I sat down on the first bench

I came to. I took out my mobile phone and tried to get my brain into gear. Who should I phone? Beri. But I couldn't. How could I tell him that Chloe had been arrested? I hadn't done what I was supposed to do. How could I tell him that I was so absorbed with trying on shoes that I had missed my cue when Chloe was leaving the shop? Granted, I didn't want to do it anyway. How was I supposed to distract people, and what if they didn't take any notice of me anyway?

Carmel.

I looked wildly around me. Beri had said that he would let Carmel loose on me like a man-eating lion to devour every shred of my being if I didn't do what he wanted. Well, I hadn't. I hugged myself and began to rock to and fro. I stifled a groan that rose up from the deepest, innermost core of my being. Carmel was going to get her wish. Beri would no longer be there to protect me and keep her at bay. He was on her side.

I had to get away. Unsteadily, I started walking through the mall. My mind was dislocated. I couldn't seem to get my thinking straight. I crashed into everyone in my path. I heard voices, but I just kept moving. Outside the mall, it was dark. I looked at my watch but my eyes wouldn't focus, the numbers seemed fused together. My legs moved of their own volition and I followed. The area wasn't very familiar to me. It didn't matter. I just felt that the more space I put between me and Beri the better I would feel.

My phone was ringing. The tone jolted me back to the land of the living. I paused for breath. Leaning against a vacant phone booth, I struggled to regain my composure. I was saturated with perspiration. My clothes were sticking to me, and sweat ran down my face. Trembling, I took the phone out of my pocket and strained my eyes to see who was calling me. I nearly dropped the phone when I saw Beri's number. It rang for a long time. When it stopped I listened to my voicemail:

'Lois, where are you? I know that something has happened to our friend. I'll meet you at your house. I'll be waiting for you.'

The small amount of strength that I had left just oozed out of me. I sagged to the ground.

'Oh, God,' I wailed over and over. 'Help me, please.'

As people were walking pass me, they gave me a wide berth. Not one person stopped to ask me what was wrong. Right there and then I needed someone, anyone, to console me. I needed guidance. I needed protection. Who could I turn to? Who?

Somehow I found the energy to stand up and get myself on to a bus. I knew that I needed to get away from the mall.

The bus stopped. The doors opened and I stepped off the platform and hurried up the street. My mind was much clearer. Lying on the floor by the phone booth in the cold had slowly engaged my mind. There was only one person that I knew I could at least talk to and that was Tia. For some reason, I couldn't remember her number. Instead, I made my way to her house. It was seven fifteen and I hoped she was in.

Only the living room had a light on. The rest of Tia's house was in darkness. I pressed the doorbell. Crossing my fingers, I hoped that she was home.

The door swung open. Tia. She was dressed for the street. Behind her were Cathy and another girl I hadn't seen before.

'Lois!' she exclaimed.

I burst into a fresh bout of tears. Relief swept over me, mingled with fear. I was relieved that Tia was home, but the fear of what was waiting for me in the shape of Beri and Carmel was strong.

'What's the matter, what's wrong?'

Cathy said, 'Tia, we'll see you up there.' Both girls came out the house. As Cathy walked pass me, she gently squeezed my arm.

Tia put her arms around me and half carried me into her house. We stumbled onto the settee. Tia flicked the table lamp on and sat down beside me. I thought that I had cried so many tears that there would never be any more. I was wrong. Tears gushed out ceaselessly. Tia got a box of tissues and I must have gone through at least half the box. She sat wordlessly, comforting me with her arm around my shoulder. My head was buried in her duffel coat. After a time, the tears did stop. My body was shaking. I was clammy and I knew that I was a bit smelly but it was a trivial thing compared to what I was facing.

Haltingly at first, I relayed the story to Tia. All the time, Tia looked at me. She didn't interrupt. She just let me speak.

'... Beri called to say that he is waiting at my house. Tia, I can't go home,' I whispered. I was waiting for her to say, 'I told you so', but she didn't. I extracted myself from her arm, and leaned back against the settee. I stared at the ceiling. It was silly really to put all my trust in Tia being able to help me. She couldn't of course, but to be able to talk about it to someone lightened the load – slightly.

'What can I say, Lois? I want to be able to help you, only I just have to work out how. But first…' She paused and looked at me. Tia bit her lip.

'What?'

'Can I pray for you?'

I was about to say no, when I thought what harm could praying possibly do? Nothing could be worse than this situation. If God would help me now, I would be more than grateful. Only I wasn't so sure that he could.

Tia prayed. She didn't say much, and I doubted whether God would hear her words. After all, God had the world to look after, and I was an insignificant girl who was just a speck of his creation. Tia's prayer didn't seem to carry any weight. I was disappointed.

I wanted her to fall to her knees, begging and pleading with tears for mercy on my behalf. Nothing doing. I brushed the prayer out of my mind – after all, to be perfectly honest, I didn't think that God was at all interested in me.

Tia had been holding my hand and she now let go.

'Right, I think you ought to phone your parents and see if it would be okay if you stayed here.' She looked at me. 'That's if you want to.'

'I do, I do.'

Mum answered the phone and when I asked to spend the night at Tia's she was a bit put out, but she knew that Tia was a 'sensible' girl and said yes.

Reclining in the bath was so soothing. Naturally, my mind replayed the happenings of the day. I thought back to when I first came to the area, the school, and met Beri. I felt so stupid. I'd been taken in by his charm.

I suppose it was because I had never really had a boyfriend before, one who knew how to pull the right strings in me to get a reaction.

Before all this happened, I saw myself as an intelligent, witty, level-headed and rational young woman. Now the picture had changed dramatically. To sum it all up in one word: fool. If I had read about a girl like me in a book or seen a play with a character in like myself, I would have scorned her. To be taken in by a guy with a nice car and money was so dense that I was finding it hard to believe myself.

That night, I lay in Tia's bed. She had given it up for me and had slept in Erica's room. She was away for the night. I had asked Tia not to tell her mum what had happened. I was ashamed to be truthful. What could her mum do anyway?

* * *

The grey morning light shafted through the curtains. I turned on my side pulling the duvet up over my head. Something didn't feel right. I sat up and I couldn't quite get my bearings. Where was I? Then I remembered – Tia's.

The clock was on top of her wardrobe facing the bed. 6.54 am. I was surprised. Normally, when I'm really stressed, I toss and turn and sleep doesn't even come near me. Yet somehow I had slept the night away. Strange, but at least I had had a good rest. My mind was much clearer.

I could smell bacon. I put on Tia's dressing gown and after I used the bathroom I went downstairs. Tia was already at the table and so was her mum.

'Morning, love,' said Tia's mum. 'Did you sleep well?'

'Yes, I did, actually.'

'Good.'

My appetite had come back, too. It had been gone for so long, and I had lost weight, and gained some spots.

The conversation was light, and I was able to push the events of yesterday out of my mind. Tia had washed and ironed my clothes. I was so touched. I couldn't imagine Sophie or any of my friends from Hartenswood doing that for me, or me for them. We didn't think on that sort of level.

Tia's mum left the table.

We were still sitting there enjoying our breakfast when she returned with her coat on.

'C'mon, girls,' she said, buttoning her coat, 'it's time for school.'

School.

The word made the mouthful of bacon I was chewing seem like cardboard. I quickly excused myself and headed for the bathroom. I spat it out, and the rest of my breakfast quickly followed.

Reluctantly I got dressed, using up the rest of my strength. I didn't want to go to school now, or ever.

17

'Lois Darnell. Would you report to Mrs Wilson's office, please?' said Ms Levine.

I had only just sat down for registration. Hurrying along the corridors, I wondered why I was being sent for. It couldn't be Beri, I thought, could it? As I neared the office I slowed down. Could it be the police? Maybe Chloe had told them that I was with her in the store yesterday, and now they had come for me. The dread of being taken away didn't appear to be a bad option to me. It was better than falling into the hands of Beri and Carmel.

I knocked on the door.

'Come in.'

Pushing the door open, I was caught off guard. Mum was sitting down, but she sprang up as soon as I entered. Mrs Crofton was sitting on one of the three chairs across this side of the desk and Mrs Wilson was on the lone chair on the other side.

'Mum!' I exclaimed, 'What are you doing here?'

'Yes, well may you ask!' she shouted. 'This, this is why I'm here.' She waved a piece of paper in my face.

'What, what is it?'

Mrs Crofton tried to calm Mum down. She didn't succeed.

'I've been working hard, trusting you to sort yourself out, and what do I find, eh? You've not been going to school. All this time I thought you were doing well. Yes, you were doing well, but not at school. Where have you been all this time?'

Mum never gave me a chance to defend myself. She ranted and raved and at one point I thought she was going to hit me. She was really angry.

Mrs Crofton swapped seats with me. She sat between Mum and me, keeping Mum at bay.

Apparently, Mum had finally received a letter saying that they were going to take her to court for my non-attendance at school.

Mrs Wilson and Mum interrogated me about why I played truant.

'You've hardly been to school, Lois,' Mum said disbelievingly.

'But it's so different from Hartenswood, Mum.'

Mrs Wilson piped up, 'Is the work too hard, dear?'

A laugh tried to escape my lips, but I held it back. 'No.' I would have loved to have told her that the work I was doing here was a breeze. But I didn't.

The two of them probed me relentlessly whilst Mrs Crofton said hardly a word. Her eyes were fixed on me, watching my every response.

I felt like a tennis ball being batted from side to side. Eventually, Mrs Wilson had had enough.

'Well, we will have to do a report Mrs Darnell, but it might be a good idea to see the school's counsellor to help present your side of the case.'

It was a dismissal.

Outside the office, Mum's face hadn't lost that angry look. I knew she wanted to say a whole lot more, but Mrs Crofton was there.

'By the way, Lois,' Mum said, 'Tony passed by the shop yesterday – *three times* – he wanted to see you.

Is he the reason for you missing school? We will speak later. Come straight home.' It was a warning. She stomped off.

Tony. Beri. Beri. Tony. One and the same person. To have come to my house three times meant that he was very angry. What was I to do? Everything I had tried so far hadn't worked, so what was left?

Mrs Crofton asked me to come to her office. I didn't want to go. I couldn't see the point, besides, I needed to think things through.

'Please come, Lois, I just want a private word with you.'

Inside Mrs Crofton's office our chairs were next to each other. She launched right in with, 'Something, or someone, is bothering you, am I right?'

I didn't answer.

'Okay. Is it Jennifer Francis and Neera Banerjee? What about Carmel Lentiss?'

I looked away.

We sat in silence for a while. Mrs Crofton said, 'Lois, I can't help you if you don't tell me anything. You're not the first girl in this school that has had problems with other pupils. But unless you let me know what is going on, I can't help you.'

Tia's voice echoed round my head: Tellhertellhertellher. But where do I begin? I thought. What would be the point in telling her? How could she keep them off of me? If, for one moment, I thought that Mrs Crofton could really help me, and it wasn't just lip service, I would tell her.

I left a frustrated Mrs Crofton in her office.

The morning drifted into lunchtime. I'd promised Tia I would meet her by the school gates.

With folded arms I leaned against the fence just outside the gates. Jennifer and Neera hadn't been in school that morning – that was nothing new. I was relieved. Whenever they were in the same class as me, I could feel their eyes on me, and was never able to take in what the teacher was saying.

A Mercedes Benz people-carrier pulled up. It was silver grey with black tinted windows.

'Lois.'

I looked up. I froze. It was Beri. He was wearing dark glasses. Although the day was grey and cold and he had no need for them, he still looked cute.

'Get in.'

I shook my head. I could see the shape of other people in the Mercedes. I guessed it was Carmel and co. I ran. Glancing behind me I saw Carmel, Neera and Anita jump out of the vehicle. Jennifer leapt out and soon overtook them. My legs picked up speed and I tore up the road. Without fear of a car accident I shot across the road. My lungs were burning up. The fear of what they would do to me if they caught me caused me to run faster.

'Lois, you're not going to get away.' Jennifer's loud voice was close.

I ran harder. I could hear her footfalls so near to me. Lowering my head I ran like the wind.

'Gotcha.'

Jennifer rugby-tackled me to the ground. We were by some shops. People were walking past, ignoring us.

'Help me, please help!' I cried breathlessly.

We were sidestepped, or stepped over by people. I could see onlookers craning their necks to see what was going on. But nobody wanted to get involved.

Carmel and Neera stood over us.

'C'mon, Jen, get her up.'

I never knew that Jennifer was so strong. She was like a man. She hauled me to my feet and spun me round to face her.

'Don't ever do that again, right?' She pointed her finger in my tearstained face. I realised then that they were determined; I might never be free.

Beri drove to us. I climbed wearily into the carrier. The girls got in behind me – all except Anita. Just as she was going to climb in, she turned and ran off.

'Oi, Anita!' shouted Carmel. 'Where you going?' Anita didn't stop to answer Carmel, she just kept running. I wished I were with her.

'Leave her and get in,' Beri said. Without looking at them or me, Beri drove off.

Jennifer, Gemma and another girl I had seen at Carmel's flat were sitting right at the back. Ellie was sitting by herself. I was squashed between the window and Neera. They were not going to let me near the door in case I took it into my head to jump out. I was that desperate I would have done, too. Carmel and Beri sat up in the front.

From where I sat, Beri and I could see each other in the mirror. He looked agitated. His eyes were hard. A shudder jolted through me. I looked away. The other girls were laughing and joking amongst themselves. Everyone blanked me. I was past caring. What could I talk to them about, anyway? The weather?

It seemed like a long drive. Beri's face was set. Whatever plans he had, I could see that he was determined to carry them out. He finally brought the

Mercedes to a halt. We were in Tralton, a leafy suburb about twenty miles from London. Beri had stopped in one of the side turnings off the high street. Everyone had stopped talking. Beri turned to look at me. The tension between us was taut. Our eyes locked. Even though I was sweating profusely, my body was cold and clammy.

Beri pointed his finger at me. 'You messed up, Lois.' His lips were tight. 'I should kill you for what you did to Chloe yesterday. She was one of my best girls.' He stabbed his finger close to my nose. 'You are going to take her place.'

The girls at the back laughed.

'Shut up,' he growled.

They did.

'Carmel, you tell her. I can't look at her – she makes me sick.'

He turned back in his seat. With relish, Carmel informed me, with a sneer on her face, of what I and the other girls had to do.

Steal.

'I can't do that. I'll give myself away before I even leave the shop.'

'That's up to you. If you want to get nicked, tough.'

My mobile phone rang. I took it out of my pocket to answer it. Tia's number was showing. Before I could answer it, the phone was snatched from me.

'I'll have that.' Carmel opened the window and flung my mobile out. Everyone laughed except me.

'Right, everyone out.' Bewildered, I looked around me. The January afternoon was bright, but cold. People were going about their business, unaware that a team of young criminals were about to descend on their neat, ordered lives. Slowly clambering out of the Mercedes I saw Beri give Gemma a cheque book. She smiled up at him, took the book, opened her bag and slipped it in.

Beri looked at me. I found it hard to find anything attractive about him. How was it that I been taken in by that ruthless, twisted smile? His eyes were like marbles – lifeless, no emotion. He took a couple of steps towards me. I moved back. Sardonically he said, 'Make me lots of money, babes. I don't want anything under fifty quid, right. If you get yourself caught you're on your own.'

At the top of the road, I looked both ways. I saw Tralton Park train station at the end of the high street to my left. I turned right. Looking in the shop windows, I could see why Beri had chosen Tralton. It reeked of money. The furniture shop, like all the other shops, had no display prices – that meant that everything was expensive. The problem that Beri hadn't foreseen was that Tralton was predominantly white. Most of the shoplifting crew were black, except Neera, who's Asian, and Gemma and Ellie who are white. We stuck out in Tralton like a sore thumb. Even as I tried to appear calm walking slowly from shop to shop, I sensed that people were looking at me.

It was 2.45. Mum was expecting me home from school in about an hour's time – there was no way that I would be able to make it. I might have called her if I had my phone, but thanks to Carmel I was phoneless. Mum would be livid.

'Poseurs' was a boutique that sold designer ladieswear. It was at least three-quarters of the way along the high street. In all this time I hadn't seen any of the others. I wondered if they had already been in here. The shop assistant was a tall thin lady with short, black dyed hair. Her ruby lips parted as she asked if she could help me.

'No, it's fine, I'm just looking.'

The clothes in the store were beautiful. Each garment boasted a top designer label. Out of the corner of my eye, I could see the shop assistant watching me. She glanced up at the ceiling a few times. There was a security camera, no doubt recording everything. I shook with fear and nerves. If I *were* able to steal anything, my every move would be recorded. A few more customers came into the shop. This was the distraction that I needed. I made sure that the camera was on my back. I tried to minimise my movements. My mind was jumping and I felt as though I was going mad. Air stuck in my throat, and it was as though my lungs were going to burst. My heart was pumping heavily and the baseline beat was thundering in my ears.

'... Stand to the left a bit, Sadie,' I heard the assistant say to one of the customers. She thought I couldn't hear her. 'The camera's not working, so I have to keep my eye on her.'

I heaved a sigh of relief to know that I wouldn't be caught on camera if I got away with it.

I was facing the window, and as I looked out I saw Beri in the Mercedes cruising to a halt not far from the shop. I was just about to slip a blouse off its hanger and under my armpit. My fingers were trembling and fumbling and a voice in my head was saying: *Take it, take it, take it.* Behind me, the assistant was chatting to another customer. I looked out the window and I saw Neera and the other girl running towards the car. Beri had the window down and he was beckoning them towards him.

What happened next was surreal. Two police cars screeched to a halt alongside Beri's Mercedes. The policemen swooped out and grabbed Neera and the other girl. I saw Gemma and Ellie being escorted by a couple of policemen and women on either side of them. Beri tried to drive off, but he only succeeded in ramming the police car. He jumped out and tried to make a run for it, but he just wasn't quick enough.

I stood with my mouth open. I dropped the blouse on the floor and walked towards the door, my mouth still open in shock. The assistant was behind me quickly, and laid her hand on my shoulder.

'Have you stolen anything from this shop?' She tightened her grip on me.

I tried to shrug her off but she was strong. 'No, and leave me alone, right?'

'Get out, and don't ever come back.'

She shoved me out the door. The commotion that the police and the shoplifting crew were causing was spectacular for Tralton. Nobody noticed me. I headed for the train station.

The train was pulling into the station as I ran down the stairs. It was a non-stop to Bempton Fords. I could get a bus to Marshton Hills from there. The carriage that I sat in was almost empty. One old guy sat at the opposite end reading a newspaper. I sat near a window. The scenery flashed past. The bare trees swayed about in the slight wind. The sky was cloudy. I folded my arms across my body and hugged myself. What an escape, I thought. My breathing had returned to normal, but I certainly didn't *feel* like me!

Seeing Beri in handcuffs made me feel sad on the one hand and happy on the other. I felt stupid to think that I had loved him. Mum was right. It was infatuation. I loved his attentiveness. The presents he gave me. His car. His manliness. Yet how come I wasn't able to pick up on his ruthlessness and the fact that he was *using* me?

'Oh, what a fool,' I whispered. Tears slid down my face. How could I be so wrong about a person? I was worth *nothing* to him. *Nothing*. He was just using me. Tia was right. Beri *was* a soul-stealer. But at least I could salvage what was left.

I felt a bit lighter. In one go, most of my problems had disappeared. Surely the gang would all be locked up for a while, which would give me time to get myself together.

The scene of the police arresting Beri and the girls replayed again and again in my mind. I was slowly allowing myself to feel relieved. But something was missing from the scene. I thought back in minute detail. Then I knew it wasn't some*thing*. It was some*one*, or rather two:

Jennifer.

Carmel.

I realised then that they were the two people that I hadn't seen being dragged off by the police.

The train pulled into Bempton Fords and the small gleam of happiness that I had allowed to swell up inside me was squashed.

Had they been arrested? Or were they still roaming around?

If they were, what would happen next?

18

'Mum took it well. Especially when I promised her that I would go to school regularly now.'

Tia was lying on my bed with her arms behind her head. I was sitting under the window in my room. It had been two days since my lucky escape and I couldn't stop talking about it.

'Tia, it was like a dream. One minute I was nearly stuffing the blouse under my arm, and would have probably got caught. Then the next it was like one of those staged TV programmes. The police car careered out of nowhere and blocked Beri's Mercedes. He had the window down and I saw the look on his face. It was indescribable. I think *he* was shocked, too.'

Pensively, Tia looked up at the ceiling.

'The thing is though, Tia, I wonder what happened to Jennifer and Carmel. Have you heard anything?'

Tia was lost in thought.

'Tia, Tia. Hello, anyone at home?!' I waved my hand to catch her attention.

She looked over at me. 'Sorry, Lois, did you say something?'

I repeated what I'd said about Jennifer and Carmel.

'No. They weren't arrested. But apparently, I heard that the police are looking for them in connection with the shoplifting spree.'

'How do the police know it was Jennifer and

Carmel? Did one of the others tell on them?'

'Oh no, thieves' honour and all that. Carmel's bag was found in the Mercedes with all her stuff and Jennifer and her were captured on camera in the shop that they were in. I've heard that they nicked over £500 worth of stuff.'

'Really?' I exclaimed.

'Whether that's true or not I don't know.'

* * *

Friday morning was my third day back at school since my narrow escape. Tia had found out last night that Beri and the others had been refused bail. Was I glad! The mystery over where Jennifer and Carmel were was still that – a mystery. But I didn't care because, as long as they didn't turn up at school, life was reasonable.

I was walking down the stairs at break-time when I saw Mrs Crofton coming towards me.

Smiling, she said, 'Glad to see you in school today, Lois. Is it possible to have a quick word with you in my office?'

My face clouded over, but I knew I hadn't done anything wrong so I said yes. Sitting facing her across her desk, I wondered if she wanted to ask me about the shoplifting episode. Everyone was talking about it. It was even on the local television news that a gang of shoplifting youths from Marshton Hills were arrested in Tralton.

'Lois.'

Mrs Crofton's voice broke into my thoughts. I turned to face her.

'Yes, Mrs Crofton?'

'I wanted to speak to you, hmm, sort of off the

record, if you know what I mean.'

Instantly, I was suspicious. I continued to look at her.

'Jennifer and Carmel and Neera are all friends, right?' She nodded at me. The hairs on the back of my neck rose up. I still didn't speak.

'The reason that I'm asking you this, dear, is that I've been wondering why you, a previously 'A' student, have fallen back in your grades and have been missing so much time from school?'

She knew. I could see it in her face. Mrs Crofton knew that Carmel and Jennifer and all the others were bullying me.

For the past few days I'd pretended that it was all behind me and that I was free to come and go as I pleased. But Jennifer and Carmel were still on the loose, and Beri and crew wouldn't be imprisoned forever. Should I tell her? What could she do for me? I wrestled with my thoughts.

Mrs Crofton stretched out her hand towards me. 'Tell me, Lois, please.'

Her eyes looked so trusting. Swallowing deeply, the memories that I had tried to bury resurfaced, bringing the same pain with them.

Haltingly at first, I told her what had happened from my very first day at Marshton Hills Community School. I didn't say anything about them press-ganging me into shoplifting with them.

I didn't mention anything about Beri, either.

Mrs Crofton came round to my side of her desk and gave me some tissues. She is the only person apart from Tia who knows my shame. I couldn't look at her. Mrs Crofton leant against her desk.

'Let me tell you something, Lois. You are not the only person that Carmel and friends have victimised. I have spoken, at length, to other pupils who were as unfortunate as you were to cross them. One of them, Samantha Taylor, is in your class.'

'Mrs Crofton,' I held up my hand to stop her from speaking. 'I'm sorry, but if you want me to speak out about them, I can't do it.'

Shaking her head, Mrs Crofton said no. 'I just wanted to know if they had been troubling you. The reason why "bullies" can escape punishment is because people are too frightened to challenge them.'

I grimaced. The thought of being bullied again in the future was horrendous.

'What can I do?' I whimpered in despair.

Mrs Crofton stood up. 'Well, you can let them plague you.' She paused. 'Or you can stand up to them.'

I left Mrs Crofton's office pondering her words.

* * *

For one whole glorious week, I enjoyed school. Tia and I walked home together. Lessons were a bit chaotic at times, but I was able to pick up some things and do my homework. Sophie phoned me on Monday evening. It was strange to hear her voice. I hadn't spoken to her for ages. After all that I'd been through, my life in Hartenswood felt like a far away dream.

'Hi, Lois,' she enthused. 'I'm really, really sorry that I haven't spoken to you for a long time. But, I refuse to take all the blame. You haven't called me either.'

Typical Sophie. If she can off-load some guilt on you, she will.

'Hi, Sophie.'

'Oh, Lois, I've met this gorgeous guy. He's a rugby player called Harry, just like Prince Harry. He's really cute. He's been living in the South of France for the past year, because of his dad's job. He lives in Hartenswood now, though. Oh Lois, I wish you could meet him. And would you believe it, he's got a twin brother and Lucy-Ann's going out with him!'

She talked non-stop about Harry and herself for half an hour! I listened out of politeness. Well, she used to be a very good friend.

There was a time when I must've been as shallow. It was sad.

* * *

The next morning was bright. Walking to school with Tia, I told her about Sophie's phone call the night before.

'… It's hard to believe that I was like that. She spent half an hour talking about *herself*! It's taken all this for me to realise that life is about much more than living for yourself. That's why people can kill and steal and do horrible things to totally innocent people, simply because they're pleasing themselves.'

'It's true,' said Tia. 'As a Christian, I feel like my life isn't my own. I have a purpose and that certainly isn't harming other people just to please myself!'

I couldn't argue with what Tia had said.

We'd reached the school gates. 'I'll meet you after school, Lois.'

'I thought we were meeting for lunch?'

'Yeah, I would've loved to, but I need to use a particular programme on the school computer to finish off some homework. Mr Raul said that he would open up the IT unit especially for me.'

During Science, Miss Frintley, the teacher, called me to one side. I had noticed that a younger pupil had slipped into the class and had spoken to her.

'Lois Darnell, could you come here, please?'

Removing my plastic protection glasses I made my way to her desk. She told me that Mrs Wilson wanted to see me.

Apprehensively, I walked quickly through the Science block to the main building and Mrs Wilson's office. What did she want me for? Had Mrs Crofton told her that Carmel had been bullying me and now she wanted me to confirm that? Mrs Crofton had said that she wouldn't tell anyone. Had she lied?

Too bad. I wouldn't say a word about Carmel if Mrs Wilson started asking questions.

I quickened my walk through the school grounds. Passing the last portacabin block, someone stepped out from around the corner. I stopped sharply and said, 'Do you mi—'

Jennifer.

Carmel stepped out behind her.

We stood looking at each other for no more than a second, but it was one of the longest seconds of my life.

Jennifer's strong hand grasped my arm tightly. I tried to pull away. It was no use. Jennifer's strength was that of a strong man's.

'Mrs Wilson is expecting me.' I hoped that that would cause them to think again.

Jennifer laughed. 'We *are* Mrs Wilson. How else do you think we could have got you to come to us, eh?'

'Dear Lois, Jennifer and Carmel would like to see

you, *now*.' Carmel laughed, then she prodded my back. 'Just do like I say, right? Otherwise you get this.' She poked me again. I was terrified. I assumed that it was a knife. Carmel's dislike for me was such that I knew she would use it too. She said, 'Come with us and shut up.'

We walked towards the Science block. I knew where they were taking me. It was to the portacabin that they used as their den. Back to square one. I hoped that Tia would be on the lookout for me again. Somehow I doubted it. We stopped outside the door. The tension was mounting.

Why did Carmel have it in for me?

What had I ever done to her?

We didn't even know each other, yet she felt this way towards me.

Jennifer pushed the door open. It hit me then that they could do whatever they wanted with me, and I would have to live with the end result of their nastiness for the rest of my life.

No.

'I'm not going in.' I stood, feet apart, trying to resist them. Jennifer stepped into the portacabin, trying to pull me in. Carmel was pushing me in the back.

Why hadn't she stabbed me yet? I realised then that whatever it was that they had planned, that wanted to do it in secret.

I screamed.

'Heeelp me!' I fought them like a wildcat. We were tussling so hard that we fell to the ground.

'Get her feet, Jen.' Carmel was breathing hard. She dropped the hairbrush that she'd been holding.

Whatever happens, I thought to myself, I must not

go into that portacabin. My arms and legs were aching, but I continued to struggle. I was fighting for my life.

Jennifer was growling, and the profanity that was flowing out of Carmel's mouth was like a bubbling sewer.

'I hate you, Lois. You think you're so nice. You think you're better than *me!*' she screeched.

'No, it's not true.'

Jennifer was astride me, pinning me to the floor. Carmel was over me, her face upside down to mine. They both paused for a moment, breathing hard.

Carmel's hair was sticking up all over the place. Her face was contorted and her eyes were wild. Hissing and spitting as she spoke, her face close to mine, she said, 'From day one I could see how you were. I hated you then and I hate you now.' She jumped up. 'C'mon, Jen, let's do her.'

My strength had seeped out of me. I gave up fighting. I shielded my face with my arms. Carmel was one hundred per cent mad. How could I win a battle against a fully-fledged psychotic?

They tried to lift me, but changed their minds. They dragged me instead. Carmel and Jennifer were getting angrier and angrier. They pushed me and pulled me, and Carmel began to hit me.

'Hey, what's going on?'

Both girls continued to assault me. Did they not hear someone call out? Or was it my ears playing tricks on me?

'Hey, you girls!'

I did hear. I took my arms from across my face. I was just in time to see Mrs Crofton get a punch in the eye from Carmel. Not wanting to be left out, Jennifer pushed Mrs Crofton with all her might. She fell backwards on the ground.

After that, it was bedlam. People seem to come from everywhere. I was lifted up off the ground and led staggering and limping towards the main building.

I was relieved that it was over – and that I was alive.

* * *

'Mum cried, Tia. I felt so awful. I was cocooned in my own world where I thought everything revolved around me. I wasn't bothered about how anyone else felt. I came first.'

We were in Tia's bedroom. I had spent the night at her house. We had spent most of the night chatting. Cathy and another friend had stayed too, but they had left in the morning to go to their Saturday jobs.

'Mind you, all this has brought Mum and I even closer together. So that's one good thing to come out of it.'

I had called Niecy and had told her the whole story. She was shocked.

'They seemed such nice girls, Lois.' I told her she needed glasses.

But something she said to me surprised me. 'You know, Lois, I thought about some of the things you said to me at Christmas, and you're right. I've been fooling myself and deep down I did like living in Hartenswood, and all the things were had there. I don't know why I was being so silly pretending it meant nothing to me when it did.'

The Saturday morning was bright. Spring would be coming in a couple of months. New beginnings.

'Most people are like that, Lois,' said Tia. 'I'm like

that at times.'

'You? But you always seem to put other people first. I don't believe you.'

Tia laughed. I tucked my arms more snugly through Tia's. We were on our way to Tia's youth group at church. The group had a netball team away match and they were a player short. I had asked Tia if I could step in. I wasn't a great netball player, but I really wanted to help Tia out. She had been a real friend to me, and even when I rejected her advice, she *still* stood by me. I just wanted to make it up to her in any and every way.

After my run-in with Carmel and Jennifer, I was a mess. Both girls were excluded from school for hitting Mrs Crofton and for attacking me. They had both been arrested for the shoplifting spree too. The whole gang would be out of action for a while, which gave me some breathing space and time to think things through. Tia said that she would be right beside me, supporting me through it.

My friend Tia. That's how I see her – as a really true, good friend. I'd never met anyone like her before. Someone who was never tired of helping me with my problems. Tia kept saying that it's 'because I'm a Christian'. I wasn't sure at first, but as I watch her living her life, I know she's got something that I haven't. Even my mum has changed. She's more considerate and loving, and no longer wrapped up in her house, car, money and holidays.

Dad, too, seems to have mellowed.

I wondered if I could have what they have. But what would it cost me?

* * *

When I thought about how I had fought Carmel and Jennifer back, I discovered something for myself.

Fear could only have as much of me as I allowed it to. If I had given up from the beginning, what would they have done to me in the portacabin? I shuddered to think.

My worse fear was being beaten up. When it happened it was frightening, but I lived through it.

Mrs Crofton said that she was so proud of me. A few weeks later she wanted to see me in her office.

'Lois, I wondered if you would be interested in a project that I want to initiate?'

I looked at her and smiled. I didn't want to get roped into something that would consume all my time, but I listened to what she had to say.

'There are so many pupils who are being bullied and who suffer in silence. I wondered – would you like to work with myself and a few other pupils in writing a school magazine, and also perhaps setting up some sort of helpline or point of contact for these pupils who don't know what to do when this happens to them?'

'I don't think I'm the right person, Mrs Crofton. Look how I was a coward and allowed myself to be involved in things that were bad.'

'Yes, dear, but you came through it all, and look at you now. I'm very proud of you.'

I wasn't too proud of myself. But I was grateful for the people around me who believed in me and hadn't given up on me.

'Okay, I'll give it a go.'

And I meant it.